T0283245

SAM CARR

ALL THE LONELY PEOPLE

Conversations on loneliness

PICADOR

First published 2024 by Picador
an imprint of Pan Macmillan
The Smithson, 6 Briset Street, London ECIM 5NR
EU representative: Macmillan Publishers Ireland Ltd, 1st Floor,
The Liffey Trust Centre, 117–126 Sheriff Street Upper,
Dublin 1, DOI YC43
Associated companies throughout the world
www.panmacmillan.com

ISBN 978-1-0350-0551-2 HB
ISBN 978-1-0350-0552-9 TPB

1 3 5 7 9 8 6 4 2

A CIP catalogue record for this book is available from the British Library.

Typeset in Scala Pro by Jouve (UK), Milton Keynes
Printed and bound by CPI Group (UK) Ltd, Croydon, CRO 4YY

Visit **www.picador.com** to read more about all our books
and to buy them. You will also find features, author interviews and
news of any author events, and you can sign up for e-newsletters
so that you're always first to hear about our new releases.

I'd like to dedicate this book to Alex, and to all of the people who allowed me to descend with them, down into their inner worlds where stories of loneliness so often reside. Your stories help us to appreciate that we are *all* the lonely people.

A Note on the Text

All the stories in this book are true. They are based upon accounts of my own experiences, the experiences of people close to me, or of people I've interviewed as part of my work over many years. To preserve their anonymity and to honour ethical guidelines, I have been careful to change names and details that might make people easily identifiable, and sometimes multiple stories are amalgamated for this purpose. In certain stories, where anonymity is not possible to preserve, full consent has been given by the person who helped shape the story.

Contents

PART THREE: Escape

PART FOUR: Outsiders

Introduction: The Crucial Thing Is the Story

There are some inevitabilities in life, like the fact that we all make mistakes, grow old and die, or that everything eventually comes to an end. I think loneliness is also an inevitability that we encounter in various guises at different points in our lives; it is not just a pathology reserved for people considered vulnerable or broken. Of course, there are infinite shades of loneliness, and how it is lived and experienced is often unique, connected to the messy constellation of circumstances that make up our individual lives. But it has a role to play in almost every life story, and, if we care to listen, stories of loneliness are all around us.

For example, take my grandpa. His own lonely and reluctant struggle with letting go of life began around a decade before he died. I can still remember, as a young man of twenty-one years old, sitting a few rows behind Grandpa in the crematorium, at Grandma's funeral. Grandma died on 1 January 2001, from the last of a series of strokes that had worn her down over several years. What distressed me most that day was the sight of Grandpa in the front row, now an old, frail man, dressed in a slightly oversized tweed suit, his thin, wispy, receding grey hair half-brushed; as Grandma's coffin disappeared behind a pair of yellow curtains, he bent over, sobbing uncontrollably and inconsolably. Some images and memories never leave you, as though they have been bookmarked.

He was beside himself, in bits, completely shattered, and in the sort of pain where it feels as though your organism just doesn't have the emotional repertoire to handle the severity of what it's being presented with. If he were a robot, I am certain Grandpa would have malfunctioned, exploding into a shower of sparks and powering down. It was possibly one of the most distressing moments of his life. Perhaps it was the formality of the occasion, or the fact that I was sitting a few rows behind him, or some kind of funeral protocol that prevented me from running up to him and holding him tightly. It seemed like the only thing that might come close to soothing him was to be wrapped up in someone's arms, in the same way a screaming, helpless, vulnerable infant is calmed when they are cradled. But I didn't do that – I'm not sure why. Maybe because it was always Grandma who played that role in our family, and she was disappearing behind a pair of yellow curtains, in a shiny mahogany box adorned with flowers.

They had been married for over sixty years and it terrified me to witness how lonely and lost Grandpa felt without Grandma. I remember thinking how life can be such an unbearably brutal bully sometimes. When they married, they probably never even thought about the eventual and inevitable ending of the union. But, as P. G. Wodehouse put it, 'in the background, fate was quietly slipping lead into the boxing glove' – a boxing glove that would eventually deal Grandpa a killer blow.[1] How on earth would he manage to redefine himself in Grandma's absence? As it turned out, he never really managed, and the next decade of his life felt like a constant struggle to stay afloat. He drifted increasingly out of touch with the world, despite our best efforts to support him. Loneliness swooped in and cast an almost permanent shadow over the final chapter of his life.

Old age was undoubtedly a major catalyst for Grandpa's loneliness during those final years. In his book *Being Mortal*, the surgeon and author Atul Gawande describes growing old as 'a continuous series of losses',[2] drawing on Philip Roth's assertion that 'Old age is not a battle. Old age is a massacre.'[3] In the decade after Grandma's death, I watched Grandpa face that massacre, struggling with the loneliness brought about by those losses. In losing Grandma, he lost the defining, most significant, protective and meaningful relationship of his life – no other relationship would ever compensate or come close. Gradually, his health and body deteriorated to the extent that he lost the capacity to engage with and reap from the world around him in the ways he had always done. He lost the sense that who he was, what he had accomplished, his narrative, or his identity, mattered. And he felt forgotten. His friends, colleagues and family members died with increasing frequency. He faced the predicament of how to exist in the world, in a meaningful sense, *without* the things and people that had empowered him to do so for most of his life. To quote one older man who recently wrote me a letter, Grandpa became one of the thousands of older people who 'stumble off into the forest, never to be heard of again'.

During this period of Grandpa's life, our paths crossed in a way I could not have predicted. I was in my early twenties and feeling lonely myself. Lucy, my first love and childhood sweetheart – for almost a decade – had left me. I'd had my heart broken for the first time and it wasn't pretty. I'd been teaching a university class as a graduate student, and I'd noticed the not-so-subtle blinking red light on my large, not-so-subtle plum-coloured Ericsson R310 mobile phone. I had a few minutes before my class started, so I picked up my phone and looked at the message. It was from Lucy.

You're probably still in bed. I wish I was there with you. I can't wait to sleep with you again, she wrote.

Huh? I thought. But she knows I'm not still in bed. I only said goodbye to her this morning, after breakfast. How can she possibly think I'm still in bed when she saw me leave? I reasoned.

Then it dawned on me that the message wasn't intended for me. And my life as I knew it came crashing down around me in those few minutes before I started teaching that class. I taught the class anyway, and when I got home our relationship ended quickly and unforgivingly. I will never forget the moment I showed her the message, like a lawyer presenting her with the indisputable evidence. She looked at it in horror, realized her error, and in an instant, it was as though there was somebody else behind her eyes. I can't explain how I knew, but I could see that all the love she had ever felt for me had drained out of her and would never return. She was somebody else now and would never again be the Lucy I knew. By default, I therefore couldn't be the same Sam. She left that very evening, and I sat in our flat with my first experience of how lonely it feels to lose your closest other.

The upshot of this was that Grandpa and I became housemates for a while, because I also had to move out of the flat Lucy and I had shared. Why not? we thought. I had nowhere to live. He was rattling around in a big house, mourning Grandma. For different reasons, we had both lost significant relationships in our lives and were both feeling very lonely indeed. The scourge of old age had taken Grandma from him, and I'd had one of my first encounters with life's many jagged edges.

Everything felt grey. What do you expect, I guess, if you put two people at different ends of the lifespan, both in the throes of grief, alone in a house together? I don't know what

Grandpa did during the day, but I had to work, and I made the two-hour round trip every day to teach classes at the university. Grandpa would be waiting for me, like clockwork, at the same time every evening. He'd be pacing around the house in his slippers, shirt and tie, and maroon cardigan, looking out of the window, waiting for me to return so that he could begin the part of the day that I know meant an awful lot to him. In truth, he didn't really come alive until around 6.30 p.m.

For the most part, our evenings consisted of the same routine. First, we would share a pot of tea and a plate of chocolate digestives in front of the fire in the living room. We sat opposite each other in large, high-backed armchairs. Neither of us ever felt like watching TV, because there were too many reminders of people who felt happy, who still had relationship partners and who we felt simply didn't understand our grief. TV isn't very sympathetic to grief, and Grandpa couldn't stand the idea of watching *Countdown* on Channel 4 without Grandma. There would be some small talk – Grandpa would ask me about my day and I'd ask him about his – but the real conversation started when Grandpa's stories and reflections began.

He told me so many stories about his life, punctuated by unusual or unexpected nuggets of information about his relationship with Grandma. I think he was trying to make sense of his life without her. One night, he'd just told me, for the umpteenth time, about when he was left stranded by his regiment on an airfield in the Burmese jungle as the Japanese army moved in. He hid in the branches of a large tree, for two days and nights, until the Japanese left and the Royal Air Force returned. As the story ended, he took an unexpected detour and suddenly decided to tell me that he could count on two hands the number of times he'd had penetrative sex with Grandma over their life. It turns out that they had been intimate about once every seven years – and two of those occurrences were more about conception, not pleasure, as Grandma took a very dim view of sex. She turned off the TV as soon as she noticed kissing, physical intimacy, or anything else she deemed to be sexually inappropriate. Grandpa admitted that evening that he had felt incredibly lonely with Grandma, in a physical sense, and had secretly longed for a level of intimacy and connection he would now be unlikely to feel before he died. I think he took the frustration and lack of sexual fulfilment to the grave.

Most evenings, we would return to the kitchen after our tea, biscuits and preliminary chat. Then, after a supper that usually consisted of one of Grandpa's meals-on-wheels (he couldn't face cooking after Grandma died), we would resume our positions by the fire in the living room and continue our conversation. At some point, I'd retire to bed, and we'd do it all again the next day. This went on for many months and I don't remember how or why I finally transitioned out of living with Grandpa. It was likely around the time I decided to do something more radical with my life and went to teach English in Russia. I do remember, however, how difficult it was for him to hide his sadness when it was time for me to move on. He readjusted his meals-on-wheels order to 'meals for one' with dignity, but we both knew that I had been a temporary life raft for him and that I was effectively leaving him to drown, alone again, in his grief.

He tried, he struggled, he cried, he grew depressed and he attempted to pull himself out of the hole into which he felt himself sinking. One year, he took a trip to Paris for Christmas. He told me he was trying to find something – something magical – that could fill the void and help him feel less alone in the world. He also told me that he didn't find it – even in

Paris. In fact, he felt more alone than ever. In those final years, Grandpa used to paraphrase something that has been attributed to Diogenes: 'We come into the world alone and we die alone. Why, in life, should we be any less alone?'

As I look back, I realize that Grandpa felt increasingly separated from the world. I sensed his terror as the 'series of continuous losses' that so often precipitates loneliness in old age caused him to drift further and further away from a meaningful connection to the world around him. There was a hunger inside him that compelled him to tell anyone who would listen what he had done with his life, why he mattered, who he was. He was trying, and failing, to fill the void created by Grandma's loss. And he was desperately trying to make sense of the baggage that inevitably accumulates over the course of a life lived.

I am an academic and a researcher. When I'm asked what I do, I sometimes call myself a psychologist, sometimes a social scientist, sometimes a human relationships scientist. But, in truth, none of these labels quite fit. It is perhaps more accurate to say that I have always been moved to look deeply into what it means to be human. Constructs such as love, loss, loneliness and human connection are prominent themes in my work and I have been privileged enough to stumble upon a career that has enabled me to explore them in people's lives. They are never easy themes to excavate because their highly subjective nature means that, to look at them deeply, others must grant you access to their inner lives.

I recently worked on a large-scale piece of research that we called the Loneliness Project.[4] My colleagues and I listened attentively to older people from across Britain and

Australia as they talked to us about their inner lives. We talked to people in many different situations: some who had yet to experience the losses and challenges my grandpa faced in his final decade, some who were currently facing those very challenges and more besides, and others who had already been through them. We were privileged to talk with these people, and we generated hundreds of hours of conversation as people willingly and openly shared their inner lives with us.

One of the things the conversations helped me to appreciate was how old age so frequently plunders people's lives, robbing them of the relationships, opportunities and resources that help countenance loneliness through the lifespan. For the most part, it was loss that seemed to be at the heart of the problem: loss of a spouse, partner, closest other, protective relationship or entire social network; loss of physical or mental capacity, or health; loss of identity; loss of meaningful connection to the world. People told us their stories of these losses and how they gave rise to an often intensified experience of loneliness.

David Foster Wallace, whom I admire greatly, had a way of bluntly articulating some of the most abstract parts of what it means to be alive. On loneliness, he argued that, in the end, 'My name's Dave, I live in a one-by-one box of bone that no other party can penetrate or know. Fiction, poetry, music, really deep serious sex, and, in various ways, religion – these are the places (for me) where loneliness is countenanced, stared down, transfigured, treated.'[5] My interpretation of this is that loneliness is a default setting in life and, if we're lucky, we may stumble upon or encounter things along the way that help us tolerate it.

In the Loneliness Project, we learned about what older people felt had helped them to countenance, transfigure or stare down loneliness. Sometimes, realizing that people had lost (or were in the process of losing) what had helped them to feel less alone over the course of their lives was a powerful lesson. As the proverb goes, you never miss the water until the well runs dry, and we talked to many people who were facing the terrifying realization that the things they had relied upon to help them fend off loneliness for most of their lives were either slowly decaying or had been quickly snatched away. We learned about how it feels when people's personal versions of the 'fiction, poetry, music, really deep serious sex, and . . . religion' were lost to them as mechanisms of relief for loneliness. What do we do when the relationship partner with whom we have shared deep and meaningful intimacy, for decades, has gone? What do we do when our bodies and health no longer allow us to interact with and appreciate what we once found in poetry, music, walking, nature, our families or whatever else has enabled us to feel less separate from the world? How does it feel when something – like old age – strips away these assets and opens the door to the winds of loneliness and isolation?

As his life faded away, I know Grandpa felt intensely lonely. I often wish that I could go back and explore his inner life during that final decade, pay more attention to how he felt, learn more about how I could have held his hand – metaphorically speaking, but perhaps literally too – through some of the challenges he faced. Sadly, I cannot go back and excavate his experiences, as they died with him. But this book is based upon a lifetime spent listening to people's lived experiences of loneliness and a desire to understand and learn from them.

As the world emerges from an unprecedented global pandemic, there has been extensive talk of loneliness as a 'pandemic within the pandemic'. It has been claimed that millions of lives have become lonelier as people's capacity to connect to each other has been restricted, revoked or limited in various ways. Often, these discussions reduce loneliness to the simple absence of social interaction. Of course, the pandemic certainly limited our capacity and opportunity to interact with others in ways that facilitate a sense of connection. But I hope that the stories and lives presented here will also demonstrate that loneliness is much more than that. Our unique experiences of loneliness cannot be fully understood without first understanding the stories behind them.

As the father of psychoanalysis, Carl Jung firmly believed people are full of stories that have not yet been told and that, as a rule, nobody knows. We are each filled with lived moments, narratives, experiences and perceptions that so often remain hidden to the world. Jung argued that his therapeutic work only really began when those untold stories were investigated. 'Clinical diagnoses are important,' he wrote, 'since they give the doctor a certain orientation. But the crucial thing is the story. For it alone shows the human background to a person's suffering.'[6]

I think that loneliness is as much personal, biographical and spiritual as it is clinical. And, as I've listened to people's stories and tried to understand what it's like to be in their shoes, I've become certain that loneliness is a part of everyone's story. It's not always easy to spot, and you have to work hard to appreciate the infinite shades of loneliness that permeate life. But, in this book, I want to share some of the touching, powerful, meaningful and impactful stories of loneliness I've been privileged enough to hear from a wide range of people over the course of my personal and professional life.

Stories need to be heard and they need someone to listen to them. One of the things I've noted most when people have told me their stories is how frequently they say, afterwards, that they feel known, understood, or that their story, or suffering, has been heard and acknowledged, often for the first time – there is something deeply comforting in that. The suffering in loneliness is often rooted to a story that has not yet been told, that remains known only to the person themselves. In the poet Della Hicks-Wilson's beautiful verse 'Small Cures', she implies that, if we are unable to open our mouths, let the truth exist somewhere other than inside our bodies, then we can be weighed down by the burden of that truth.[7] What remains unspoken, remains inside us, and, when stories of loneliness are unshared, untold and unexplored, they can make us ache all the more. As the English scholar Terry Lee suggested, our stories should be honoured with compassionate listening that in turn catalyses new possibilities for empathic connection and understanding.[8]

I hope the true stories in this book reinforce the fact that loneliness isn't something that only happens to unfortunate other people. Stories and experiences of loneliness are all around us. They are reflected in things and people we have lost, or perhaps never found, in what surfaces within us when we are alone with ourselves, and in our capacity and willingness to allow others access to the largely impenetrable internal worlds we are forced to inhabit as humans. Just because we aren't feeling lonely now does not mean we won't someday, as the stories and scripts of our lives unfold.

PART ONE

RELATIONSHIPS

The Nurse, the Driver, the Carer, the Cook and the Bottle Washer

As we sat in her living room with a cup of tea and a digestive biscuit, Paula, aged seventy-two, wept as she tried to describe the immensity of the challenge she had faced since the death of her husband, Bob, four years ago. She had been Bob's carer for over ten years, as he slowly declined from a degenerative condition. She told me that she was 'his nurse, driver, carer, cook and bottle washer'.

On the wall opposite me hung dozens of photographs, framed and neatly arranged in symmetrical rows. I noted their wedding photograph. Bob looked young, fit and healthy as he smiled into the camera with his arm around Paula. As the photographs appeared to move through the decades, though, Bob looked increasingly unwell. In one picture, he was sitting in his wheelchair, emaciated but smiling and holding a glass of champagne, as Paula sat beside him with her arm around him. She frequently glanced at the photographs as she talked.

'You are almost invisible, you know. You kind of live in the shadows, as the carer,' she told me. 'For the first four years after Bob died, I couldn't have cared less whether I was alive or dead. I didn't bother to do anything.' She paused. 'I loved him. The only way I can describe it to you is, while he was alive and I was his full-time carer, companion, friend, we had a ball – even though he was in a wheelchair. But, when he was gone, I didn't know where I fitted any more. I didn't know who I was any more, because I wasn't . . .'

Paula could not finish her sentence and she burst into tears. She just 'wasn't' any longer. That was the truth about how she had felt since Bob's death. She was overcome with the emotional impact of hearing herself say it. Weeping seemed to convey her feelings far more appropriately than any attempt to verbally articulate them. We both implicitly knew this. We also both knew that her excavation of her own feelings had hit upon the crux of the issue – she did not know where she fitted in the world any longer. Without Bob, she did not yet know how to rediscover a meaningful sense of connection to the world around her. Refracted through the unique lens of Paula's internal world, I sensed in her the sort of loneliness my grandpa had experienced all those years ago, and I felt a deep sadness. I remember looking at the teapot on the table, and the plate of digestive biscuits, and I was transported back to the living room where I had sat with Grandpa, listening to him struggle with some of the very same demons.

Alice, another interviewee, was eighty-eight years old. She had a frail appearance, and one of the first things I noticed when we talked was her tendency to call me 'dear' or 'deary' almost every time she addressed me. It didn't feel condescending or patronizing. I rather liked it because it reminded me of how my grandma had spoken to me as a child. Alice had lost two husbands and her entire family, including siblings, most of her friends and her only son. She also had some challenging health issues to contend with. She told me that, not so long ago, she had awoken in hospital after a bad fall, and regretted the fact that she'd woken up. She spoke with a calm soberness as the sun shone through the open patio doors of her small retirement apartment.

'I don't have any relationships, dear,' she told me. 'They've all died. And, you know what? Underneath it all, I wouldn't mind leaving this world. Everyone has died and I think I'm lonely.'

She paused, looking out at the garden. Then, leaning a little closer to me, as though she was telling me a secret, she continued, 'I'm not remarkable, dear. But shall I tell you what I am?' she smiled. 'I'm strong. I'm so strong that I can admit to myself and to you that there's nothing left for me here. I'm more than ready to leave when it's my time.'

Up to that point, I hadn't seriously considered what it might feel like to lose *everyone* you'd ever felt close to.

Some years later, I remembered the look of sincerity in Alice's eyes as she leaned over and told me that life had lost almost all of its meaning and death seemed like a more palatable alternative. The look had left me in absolutely no doubt that she was serious. I was in Belgium with my colleagues Chao and Jana, from the Centre for Death & Society at the University of Bath, discussing the concept of 'tiredness of life' in older people with a network of Dutch, Belgian and Swiss geriatricians, gerontologists, physicians, psychiatrists, social scientists and palliative care specialists. We were discussing whether some older people, like Alice, are genuinely 'tired of life' to the extent that they should have the right to euthanasia if they feel that living has become little more than irreversible and permanent suffering.

As we listened to experienced colleagues from countries where law and policy permits a more liberal perspective on such issues, I heard case studies and experiences of older people that convinced me that many *do* reach a point where they are so 'tired of life' that death is a most welcome visitor. We wrestled inconclusively with what precisely the phrase *means*, and it seemed to me that, while certainly not synonymous with age-related loneliness, the concepts were nonetheless bedfellows. That is, almost all older people who are genuinely 'tired of life' seem to report an associated sense of feeling completely disconnected from the world due to the cumulative effects of the losses and ravages of ageing.

Dr Helena Larsson and her colleagues at Malmö University in Sweden have documented a process in older people nearing the end of their lives that they liken to a gradual 'turning out of the lights'.[1] They argue that people steadily let go, losing their physical capabilities and relationships until they get to a point where they are ready to turn off the outside world. When I first read Larsson's work, I was reminded of the admittedly disputed myth of the elephants' graveyard, which fascinated me as a child – and still does. According to the legend, the elephants' graveyard is a place where older elephants instinctively go in anticipation of death. Lured by some spiritual or supernatural force that cannot be explained by natural laws, the older elephants, realizing that their journey is coming to an end, separate themselves from the world that anchored them to life, and take a long walk towards death. They make a decision to face it alone, far from the herd, and in a way that does not hinder the progress of those that remain behind. There is logic in the idea of letting go of life to face death. It makes sense to gradually loosen our grip before we finally let go. I wondered if that was what had happened to Alice.

But my experiences as a researcher have led me to believe that, for human beings, this process is sometimes very different from the romanticized notion of the elephants' graveyard. As David Foster Wallace put it, 'everything I've ever let go of has claw marks on it'. Just because it makes sense to let go of something, it does not mean it is easy, quick or painless. In Grandpa's case, I remember that gradually losing or letting go of the things and people that had helped him feel less alone in the world didn't feel like a kind or compassionate process, and it happened with an inevitability and brutality that challenged him in ways you couldn't describe as anything other than cruel. I often think about whether Grandpa would have opted to turn out the lights sooner if he'd lived in a society where such an 'out' was an option.

As Chao, Jana and I – both colleagues and friends – sat at the dinner table after a long day of discussions in Belgium, we pondered some of the broader connotations of 'tiredness of life'. Chao is from China and was able to offer particular insights into the concept from a Chinese perspective.

'You see, in China, suffering from "tiredness of life" wouldn't be seen as a reason for euthanasia,' Chao told us.

There were big questions to consider, like whether someone who is genuinely *suffering* from something like 'tiredness of life' should have the right to choose death. How would you know, for instance, that things might not take a turn for the better? Or that an older person who felt that they were 'tired of life' – and had an unwavering wish to die – might not experience some sort of 'epiphany' or 'rebirth' if they just waited a little longer or received appropriate help and support? Was 'tiredness of life' not something younger people could also experience? Or was there something unique about 'tiredness of life' in old age? Were there conditions that resembled 'tiredness of life' but were distinct and treatable psychiatric issues?

'You see, in China,' Chao continued, leaning back in his seat and scratching his head, 'even your death doesn't *belong* to you. Your death, just like your life, also belongs to the collective – to your country, to your family, to your people – so, even if you're "tired of life", that doesn't give you the right to end it. That's how people in China would see it.'

Jana commented that it was a wonderful way to turn the argument on its head, but I still had some thinking to do. And Paula had popped into my head too. Her struggle with grief and loneliness had undoubtedly made her tired of life. I wondered what she'd say about all of this.

I talked with Paula for almost three hours before our conversation drew to a natural conclusion. At this point, she wanted to make me a sandwich and a cup of tea. She went to the kitchen, looked in the fridge and asked me whether I would prefer ham or cheese, and whether I wanted an apple or an orange to accompany it. I politely replied that an apple and a ham sandwich would be lovely.

As we ate our sandwiches, Paula told me that she felt lighter. She said that she hadn't had much opportunity to talk to anyone about the things we had talked about that day. She hadn't had the chance to tell the story of Bob's death, what it meant for her, what she had lost, how she had grieved, where it had left her, how alone she felt and how she had struggled to rediscover a meaningful sense of connection to the world. Over lunch, I felt as though we were closer to each other simply because of the conversation we'd shared. She told me that, for the first time, it felt like someone outside of her own head knew about the story of her suffering, and there was clearly something deeply comforting about that for her.

Paula wanted me to know that she had started to feel as though small shoots of hope were emerging.

'Well, I'm fortunate. I know everybody would say, "Oh, how awful," or whatever, after your partner has died, but when you can actually get to grips with what your life might become, even at my age, the freedom is one of the best things,' she told me.

'Don't get me wrong – I've been in hell for the last four years and I wish to God I hadn't,' she continued. 'But if, and when, you can get past that bit – the hell, the emotional torment and the upset – for the very first time in my life, I'm able to do what I want to do. I've always had to "do" for someone else, or "because" of someone else, or "about" someone else. But now, I have to say, I'm just starting to notice that there's a little thrill to being able to do exactly as I please, and if people say, "Oh, but you *should* . . ." I go, "No, I *shouldn't!*"' She laughed.

Carl Jung wrote about the *mortificatio*, which he believed was an essential part of the 'work of life'.[2] The *mortificatio*, he argued, is a time of rebirth, a time that will always be preceded by torment because something *must* die or be lost in order to be reborn. But he also believed that there was a 'secret happiness' awaiting us on the horizon when we eventually step out of the darkness that inevitably follows loss. I like to think that's what Paula was trying to tell me as I finished my ham sandwich.

The Lost City

It's difficult for me to remember a time when I felt that my parents really expressed any sort of love towards each other. When I sift through my memories of their relationship, most of what I recall is a collection of traumatic, chaotic arguments, fights, disharmony and disconnection. I feel bad saying that, slightly guilty; I feel it would hurt them to know that's how I remember things. Because, like most of us, they were good people, doing their best with the limited relational tools they'd been dealt. I'm not saying they *didn't* love each other, somewhere underneath it all, but there was just too much anger, resentment, fear and pain that had built and built over many years, until the love was sort of irretrievably buried, like a lost city underneath a pile of volcanic ash. That's how some relationships end up.

Like individuals, I think most couples have a public persona, the face of the relationship that is presented to the world. This persona can differ markedly from what plays out behind closed doors. My parents' relationship had a fun, buoyant face: boozy summer barbecues with friends, giggly parties and a fun-loving atmosphere. They were life-and-soul, die-hard members of a local brigade who regularly hosted get-togethers on weekends. However, the relationship tended to play out differently when life asked for more than a game of pétanque, a barbecued sausage and a crate of Stella Artois. That's when the uglier side came out to play.

Dad had his first affair when I was around five years old.

As it turns out, he was sleeping with one of Mum's best friends. I remember how, one chilly winter evening, Mum seemed particularly on edge as she drove us to the car park of a lively looking pub. Dad was supposed to be playing darts that night, but I think darts had been a cover for the fact that he was meeting 'her'. I remember him coming out of the pub in flares and a tight T-shirt, leaning into the car window, and my parents having an emotionally charged argument about the fact that he was 'lying through his teeth', 'still seeing "her"', and should collect his stuff and 'get out of the house'. Mum was crying as she told Dad that he should say goodbye to us kids because it was the last time he would see us. With that, we screeched out of the car park, Mum's erratic driving reflecting her emotional state. I cannot remember exactly how I felt, tucked up in the car, wearing a duffle coat over the top of my pyjamas, with my little brother Joe and sister Em beside me. I must have been afraid or distressed, but the only thing I remember is wondering whether we might crash.

As it turned out, it wasn't the last time we saw Dad. We saw him the very next day, in fact. Apparently, he climbed into the bedroom window that night and somehow reinserted himself into Mum's life. I'm not sure she ever completely forgave him for the affair, and I don't think either of them ever did the necessary work in relation to the wounding, healing, understanding, forgiveness or compassion that is necessary to even begin to overcome the depth of the attachment wounds things like infidelity inflict on a relationship. It marked the beginning of two long decades of building resentment, anger, emotional distance and relational discord. She couldn't forgive him, and resented him more and more deeply as time went by. He distanced himself, buried his head in the sand, became a stranger and resented the fact that she resented him.

For what seemed like years, there was a pattern to family life. Every evening, Dad would come home late from work, on account of the fact that he'd been to the pub. Sometimes, he would resist staying at the pub until closing time and he'd come home at around eight or nine o'clock in the evening. At other times, he would stagger through the front door at around eleven-thirty or midnight, having waited for last orders. Invariably, he had drunk more than he should have, and a similar, predictable course of events would take place every night, like clockwork.

At the sound of his key in the lock, Mum would jump out of her chair like a coiled snake, having waited patiently for her prey. As she asked him where he had been, and in particular whether he had been to the pub, she could barely conceal the anger and distress in her voice. Sometimes, she already knew the answer, because we'd seen his dark grey Alfa Romeo Spider parked outside the pub on our way home from a friend's house or an after-school club. She was simply testing his capacity to tell the truth. Dad would either tell her that he *hadn't* been to the pub – a rather pointless barefaced lie – or, when he was thinking more clearly, he'd say that he'd 'just popped in for a quick pint with Richard Ellis'. Using language like 'just' and 'popped in' and 'quick pint' was his way of making it all seem like no big deal, as though he were doing something like picking up a pint of milk from the shop on his way home. I guess he was trying to minimize the damage, but was making a pretty bad fist of it.

Next, Mum would ask to smell Dad's breath as further corroboration. She would lean into the cubic foot of space in front of his face and take a long, deep inhalation. Invariably, he stank of booze – you could smell it the moment he walked in the door. She'd tell him he was a liar and that she couldn't believe he had such little regard for her or his family. The

living-room floor, near to the TV. As far as I remember, things went on like that for years.

They were both lonely, probably much lonelier than they would ever have been had they not imprisoned themselves in their relationship. Mum cried alone upstairs for many, many nights. As I got older, I felt increasingly compelled to comfort her, and, in many ways, I became her emotional confidant. I would go up to her room when I returned from evenings out with my friends, sit on the bed beside her and listen, offering her a space to talk about how she was feeling, before retiring to bed myself. Effectively, Dad became a bit of an alien in our family home. He completely withdrew, never came on family trips to visit relatives, nor to school parents' evenings. He didn't seem like a presence that was valued, welcome, which made him stop wanting to be there at all. He felt a bit like an unwanted rodent who lived in our house, raided the kitchen cupboards during the night, and whose presence caused a great deal of anxiety and turmoil. But I am sure he must have felt isolated, abandoned and like an outsider in his own home. I can't imagine how difficult that must have been for him.

One night, when I was about seventeen, Dad came home at around midnight and the same old argument ensued. I heard it from my bedroom as I was settling down to sleep. I knew that things got pretty heated sometimes, so I decided I would wander into the living room, just in case a referee was required. Dad was right in the middle of the room, standing underneath the chandelier, glistening with the sweaty sheen – a bit like the sheen on a snail or slug – that always appeared on his skin when he'd had too much to drink. Mum was standing in front of him, angry and extremely animated. It was like watching an excitable hare in an altercation with an enormous intoxicated snail. I walked in, but it was as though I was invisible to them; they were so engrossed in the argument that I don't think they even noticed me.

When her anger and desperation became too much, Mum could become a little threatening and invade Dad's personal space. That's exactly what happened that night. He had never hit her, and I don't think he would have done so that night either, but I noticed something snap inside him and he roared, a bit like a crazy, angry bear, and lunged forwards. Instinctively, I stepped between them and pushed him backwards, assertively, telling him that was 'enough'. He was intoxicated and unsteady on his feet, and he fell backwards against the wall. As he fell, he looked up at me and our eyes met for a second. I knew from the look in his eyes that he felt hurt, emasculated and cut adrift. Then everything stopped and went silent. Dad just lay on the floor, looking up at the ceiling, for what felt like an eternity; Mum ran upstairs crying, and I stood there, feeling as though time had stopped. Then I followed Mum, to make sure she was OK.

I cried that night in my room. The moment gave rise to many different shades of loneliness inside me that I couldn't cope with all at once. I felt as though I had pushed Dad further into the desert and further away from me. It was as if I'd scared off a wild animal I had been desperately trying to befriend and had hoped would find its way to me. I felt like, metaphorically speaking, I'd thrown a great big rock at him, made loud noises and told him to skedaddle. I was scared I had chased an already distant figure in my life even further away.

They call it 'parentification' when a child takes on responsibility for the tasks, duties, safety or emotions of their parents to preserve family peace. Such children are inadvertently drawn into becoming part of the parental subsystem. That night, I had effectively refereed, intervened in and emotionally negotiated an out-of-control playground squabble between two small children – but they were my parents. And, in the aftermath, while one of them was upstairs sobbing and the other was lying intoxicated and wounded on the living-room floor, I found myself in desperate need of an older, wiser, safe, secure other to help me deal with the emotional turbulence inside *me*. Somewhere, not so far from the surface, I wanted someone to hold me, soothe me and help me regulate my own feelings about what had just happened.

They lived like that – Mum and Dad – for so many years. I can't imagine that they were ever happy, and I think they thought they were doing us children a favour. They were one of those couples who stayed together 'for the sake of the kids'. It all finally ended abruptly when it was brought to light that Dad had failed to pay his income tax for years and owed the Inland Revenue large amounts of money. We had lived in Cobbler's Cottage for such a long time, it was our childhood and family home, but the debt, which Mum knew nothing about, had to be paid. They were forced to put the house up for sale. I think that was the final straw for Mum. She left him when the house was sold, and they went their separate ways. That was when our family exploded from the pressure that had built up over many years; like subatomic particles, we fractured and ricocheted off in different directions. I remember, as we packed up the last of our belongings from the place that we had called home, Dad broke down, wept and begged for Mum's forgiveness. I think it was the first time I genuinely felt that maybe, underneath it all, he really did love her. But by then it was far too late.

Now, when I visit Mum during summer holidays or at Christmas, I always feel a powerful urge to drive past Cobbler's Cottage. I eagerly point out my old home to my thirteen-year-old son, Alex, as we slow the car down to take a long, hard look. I recognize the large garage Dad built at the front of the house, the huge garden at the back, my sister's old room, the front door and the living room, where, all those years ago, that emotionally charged incident took place. I no longer feel any anger or resentment towards my parents for the relationship they endured and the ways in which it sculpted some of my and their experiences of loneliness. I would be lying if I said that I haven't felt angry in the past, but time, therapy and the realization that we are all human help. As the psychoanalyst James Hollis argued, 'Many of us had wounded parents who could not meet all of our needs for nurturance or empowerment. I have heard it said that psychotherapy is about blaming parents for one's miseries or suffering.'

He continues: 'Quite the contrary. The more sensitive we are to the fragility of the human psyche, the more likely we are to be able to forgive our parents for being wounded and woundable.'[3]

Loneliness finds its way into most childhoods, in one way or another. Despite that, I love my parents and I am grateful to them both for the gifts they have given me.

Zak and the Miracle in the Kitchen

Some children are born into a world completely devoid of positive caregiver relationships in all senses. This was Jake's reality. He was ten when we met him. He had grown up in foster care after being removed from his home due to severe neglect and abuse on the part of his biological mother and her partner. His biological father had never been on the scene. The foster agency informed us that Jake had been placed in seven different homes in the last five years because he was a 'difficult' child. He was now so afraid of being relocated that the first thing he did when he got home from school each day was run upstairs and check whether his belongings were still in his room. He expected and deeply feared being packed up and shipped out, which he felt could happen at any moment.

Understandably, Jake didn't trust the succession of either incapable or well-meaning adults who had been charged with caring for him since birth. He was now living with Trudi, a single foster carer who lived alone with her dog, Zak, in a terraced house somewhere near Sheffield. Jake had been placed with Trudi because a previous family had decided they simply couldn't cope with him after around six months. He didn't trust Trudi either, and why should he?

'I still find it hard being really close with Trudi, 'cos everyone in the past has been horrible to me, and eventually absolutely everyone has got rid of me. There's still a chance that Trudi might do that, so I don't feel safe with her. No way,'

Jake told us, as he sat at the kitchen table, eating a packet of crisps.

'Maybe I would feel safer if I were, like, adopted or something, but I'm in foster care, see, which is why the social worker comes around and checks on me, 'cos they, like, own me, or something. The problem is that nobody wants to adopt me so I can live there all the time without having to move to new homes,' he explained, licking the cheesy, salty residue from his fingers in a way that suggested the crisps were far more important to him than the conversation. I wondered whether his nonchalance was a defence against the fact that we were talking about a painful issue.

Jake was a participant in another project we'd conducted a few years ago that sought to explore the inner experiences of children in foster care. The children's profiles and case notes made for sobering reading. Like Jake, they had each spent somewhere between five and ten years in the foster system and, on average, had moved homes between six and ten times. Their reasons for being in foster care were parental neglect and abuse, or parental death. They were struggling to build positive and warm relationships with their foster families, and most had completely lost faith in adults as a genuine source of safe, secure and consistent love and affection. It makes for a different shade of loneliness when, like Jake, you've never known what it feels like to have a genuine, trustworthy, warm, affectionate, consistent and secure attachment to a caregiver. That's when your internal world begins to evolve around beliefs like 'I'm unlovable', 'I can't trust anyone', 'They'll all let you down in the end', 'It's pointless getting close to people', or 'I hate myself and others'. That's where Jake was at.

But we learned from Jake that, even amid such a desolate attachment environment, we still manage to find ways to satisfy our innate need to feel safe and not so alone. 'I don't mind being really close with Zak [the dog] though, 'cos he won't get rid of me. I do feel really safe with him,' Jake told us. 'I think he's my friend because he wants to be and not just because he has to be.'

Zak was a six-year-old golden retriever. He was calm, gentle and had a sort of caring wisdom about him that some dogs exude. We quickly realized that Zak's role was paramount in helping Jake to feel less alone in the world and in helping him learn to trust Trudi. Jake opened up to us about the important role Zak played as the only living creature on earth who could help him feel less alone, especially in relation to his lack of control over having a place to call home.

'I used to hide in the living room with Zak when there was a knock at the door. I used to worry it was the social worker coming to take me away. I didn't feel safe without him and, when I was with him, just holding his ears, I felt relaxed and I wouldn't have the big thumping feeling in my body,' he explained.

Sometimes, to feel less alone when we're drowning in feelings of terror and vulnerability, what psychologists have called 'contact comfort' is vital – we need skin-to-skin contact with a safe, warm, living other.

That day, Jake told us that he often felt afraid and alone at night, and the intensity of his feelings frequently prevented him from sleeping. He described how, one night, he had wandered into the dark hallway in his pyjamas and peered through the banisters into the kitchen below. He saw Trudi's silhouette. She was doing the washing up and Zak was sitting beside her, looking up at Trudi as though he was listening attentively to what she was saying, like a wise old sage.

I don't have strong religious beliefs, but, as Jake recounted the story, the image in my mind was like a picture of the Nativity scene I remember from an old Advent calendar I had as a child. In the image, you were looking through the stable doors onto the birth of Jesus. Everything in the picture was dark: the night, the stable interior and the hills in the background. But, inside the stable, around the birth scene, there was this powerful, focused light that was incredibly intense and in such stark contrast to the darkness all around. You could see the three wise men, the shepherds, Mary and Joseph, the baby Jesus and a plethora of farm animals. The whole scene just lit up and shone miraculously out of the dark stable. This is how I pictured Jake's miracle in my mind, as though he was looking into the kitchen, in a dark house, on a dark landing, on a bleak night, in a bleak town, as the silhouette of Trudi and Zak doing the washing up beamed out at him, illuminated by the fluorescent tube light that was just a little too bright.

Trudi had been talking to Zak. Jake hadn't found it odd that she was talking to the dog – after all, he talked to Zak more than anyone. Zak was, in fact, the only one he really trusted. It wasn't the fact she was talking to the dog that made his heart thump. It was what she said that was so powerful, for him, he told us. What he heard made him feel a deep thumping in his body; his heart was pounding so hard that he almost shook.

While she was washing up, Trudi had told Zak that she 'liked having Jake around'. She said that she thought he was a 'lovely boy' and that she 'hoped he would be around for a long time to come'.

'Nobody has ever said that about me,' Jake exclaimed. It excited and terrified him in equal measure to think that Trudi felt that way about him. Jake had never experienced what it felt like to be wanted before. He had never experienced the sense that someone wanted him around, cared about him, or liked him. And, strangely, hearing it in secret, eavesdropping in the hallway, made it all the more credible. Trudi wasn't saying it to make him feel better. How could she be? She didn't even know he was listening. But what she said to Zak that night shook the little boy's world and opened him up to the idea that it just might be possible to be wanted.

I think Jake's story demonstrates that hope springs eternal where childhood attachment is concerned. Even when life is incredibly challenging, as it undoubtedly was for Jake, there are shoots of hope that offer unexpected pathways out of loneliness. Eventually, Jake would slowly begin to open the door to Trudi, and Zak was a major part of that process. Jake was a bit like a little scientist in those first few months with Zak and Trudi. It was as though he wandered around with an imaginary clipboard, collecting empirical evidence that Trudi could be trusted and would not hurt him. One day, he looked up at us sincerely and spoke with the authority of a scientist presenting compelling data at a conference. He gave a brief but impassioned speech.

'Look, she takes real good care of Zak – *all the time* – and never gets angry or fed up with him. She is really nice to him, and always makes sure he's OK. I think maybe I was wrong about Trudi. Zak *must* love her, and *he* wouldn't do that if she wasn't nice.'

It was as though he had logical proof: if *Zak* had decided Trudi was nice, then it necessarily followed that she *must* be nice. Our project taught us that family pets can be an enormously important part of the fostering process. Pets like Zak seemed to help children like Jake learn to trust other members of the family. Psychologists might call Zak a 'transitional being', helping to soothe and divert Jake's anxieties about human-to-human relationships until a trusted rapport can be established. Zak was simultaneously a port in a storm for Jake and a bridge or broker in relation to the development of trust between Jake and Trudi.

'It Never Gets Better'

Frank gripped the sides of his beige tartan recliner, avoided eye contact and looked at the floor as he spoke. Despite his age, he reminded me of a tough schoolboy trying to maintain the impression that his armour was impenetrable and that he could handle anything that was thrown at him. He rarely said more than a single sentence at a time, and what he said was delivered with a steely, defensive quality that made me feel reluctant – maybe a little afraid – to challenge him or ask him to elaborate. There were times when I felt frustrated by his monosyllabic answers and I wondered why he had volunteered to talk to me in the first place – it felt as though he didn't want to be there.

This is how I sometimes experience interactions with my son, Alex, when he gets into the car, after school, at five minutes past three. It's a common experience for parents. I show interest in his school day, his life and what he's been up to, but my genuine curiosity is typically met with a barrage of short, sharp, blunt responses, delivered in a way that lets me know that it is not welcome. If I push on with my attempts to ignite a conversation, I'm sharply told that I shouldn't ask such things immediately after a tiring day at school, and, 'I'll share when I'm ready, OK?' Unexpectedly, I felt something similar with Frank, but I pushed on regardless.

Frank lived in a retirement community on the outskirts of a large Australian city. He was eighty-seven years old and spoke with a thick Australian accent, which he must have

acquired since emigrating to Australia with his wife, Margaret, and their family in 1966. I noted that he was much
more comfortable talking about the factual details of his
life than about how he had experienced it or how he felt
about it.

Frank was born and grew up in London. He was one of
seven siblings. 'There were the twins at first, then my elder
brother and then me,' he explained.

'So, were you close to your mother?' I asked.

'Not really. I wasn't close to her,' he replied.

'What about your father?' I continued.

'He was my father.'

'Did you feel close to him?' I asked.

'No,' he responded tersely. 'I don't know what your family
was like – but, in mine, children were seen and not heard.
It's always been that way for me.'

It felt like Frank had spent his life being seen and not
heard. From the outset, he seemed to have received the message that what he felt and experienced had no relevance to
anyone, and so he'd built his relational life on an unwritten
script that simply didn't take account of other people's feelings or expect them to take account of his. I asked about the
people in Frank's life he felt close to, the people he might
confide in when he needed support.

'I don't confide in anybody,' he said. 'I don't talk to
anybody.'

Frank left school at thirteen and started working as a van
boy, delivering groceries off the back of a horse and cart. He'd
married Margaret when she was just sixteen years old and he
was twenty-two. At that time, he worked as a scaffolder, and
he'd had a string of manual-labour jobs ever since. He had
worked as an electrician, as an employee in a Land Rover
factory, and in a company making neon signs, back 'when

they first came onto the scene'. He and Margaret had been married for fifty-nine years when she died, five years ago, of a heart attack. They had five children. I asked whether he felt close to his children.

'No,' Frank replied.

'Was Margaret close to them?' I continued.

'I wouldn't know,' he responded, his accent thicker than ever.

It was clear that Frank had neither grown up in, nor built, a family where it was considered the norm to talk about, express or reveal feelings about anything. I asked whether it was important to him that he could be there for his children in an emotional sense.

'No. They're the same as me,' he replied. 'Emotional issues, medical challenges or concerns, problems, money worries – I wouldn't know a thing about it. It's not on the agenda in our family.'

Looking for a soft underbelly somewhere, I asked whether Margaret had been more sympathetic to such issues.

'Nope. Same as me,' he replied. 'Maybe a tiny bit more loving.'

There was clearly powerful emotional indifference in the family environment Frank described. At some point, I asked him whether he felt Margaret enjoyed her life.

'I never asked,' he responded. 'We never asked what each other enjoyed or didn't enjoy.'

Frank reminded me of a slightly harsher version of my dad. It was the aloofness, the absence of emotional language or expression, and the sense that I was trying to get blood from a stone that felt familiar. But eventually Frank showed me that stones bleed too. His vulnerability and personal feelings of loneliness eventually began to surface, and they

revolved around losing Margaret, who had been his companion for almost sixty years of life.

'It must have been a very difficult time for you, Frank,
losing Margaret,' I ventured.

'Why?' he replied.

'Well, I think it's very hard losing somebody we love.'

'It hasn't stopped being difficult, you know.'

I felt a distinct change in his voice, and I instinctively
knew he was about to reveal something vulnerable.

'No, I'm sure it hasn't,' I said softly. 'Five years is not so
long ago, is it?'

'No. They say it gets better. But it never gets better . . .'

'It's OK, Frank,' I said, as I sensed that what he was feeling wasn't easy for him.

'Don't EVER say it gets better; it never . . .'

At this point in the conversation, Frank was confronted
by the painful void inside him that he had been burdened
with since Margaret's death. He didn't have much of a platform from which to express these feelings – he hadn't yet
allowed himself to reveal them or to ask for support – but,
somewhere inside, he felt a deep sense of emptiness at losing
the only true companion he'd ever known. Margaret had
been, as he put it, his 'right arm'.

'Can we have a break for a minute? Do you want a cup of
tea?' he asked. So, we drank tea while he, suddenly softening,
showed me photographs of Margaret.

Tea facilitated almost every conversation we had in the
project. It tirelessly comforted people when the need arose,
and allowed for a peaceful, restful and safe environment for
often difficult conversations. For that, I am truly thankful for
tea.

*

Over half the people we talked to in the Loneliness Project had, like Frank, lost a long-term partner or spouse. Warm, protective, meaningful, dependable and loving bonds are one of our main sources of protection from loneliness. But a cruel irony of life is that such relationships are neither handed out like candy nor evenly distributed. There are two main ways that the absence of such meaningful and enduring attachments seems to give rise to loneliness. The first is the sort of loneliness we encounter when we are unable to *find* such relationships in the first place, when the people we might have built them with are, for whatever reason, unable to be a part of them. These relationships are often desolate from the beginning and are accompanied by a pervasive sense of loneliness emanating from the fact that something is missing – because it is. The second is the sort of loneliness experienced when we have been lucky enough to stumble upon a meaningful, protective, safe, secure, dependable attachment to someone we love – or even an imperfect, unsatisfactory one that isn't always secure, satisfying or rewarding, but that we rely upon nonetheless – only to *lose* it to the inevitability of death. This sort of loneliness is strongly characterized by the crippling grief we experience when we lose someone or something we were deeply attached to.

We published the early findings from the Loneliness Project in the mainstream media. In one article, we presented snippets of data and first-hand accounts of what people like Frank had shared with us. People seemed to recognize reflections of their own personal experiences and struggles, and often reached out to us. Perhaps the project legitimized or helped them voice their experiences. I received an anonymous message from a man who had recently lost his wife of forty-five years, and it deeply moved me.

Thank you for this important research, which resonated powerfully with me, as my wife of forty-five years died a year ago today. I have also lost my parents and my brother. Although those losses were hard, they pale in comparison to the loss of my wife. This is because with her death I lost her intimate companionship, which had nurtured me for nearly half a century. I have things to do around the house and garden. But it all bears the imprint of the taste and artistic nature of my wife, which I do not want to lose. I am still surrounded by her things. I will keep many of them, including some of her favourite clothes. I want to keep remembering her. I still think of her every single day. Every grief experience is unique, but I do think that, as this article points out, supporting the loneliness of the grief-stricken is vital.

The loneliness of grief struck me powerfully in many of our conversations with older people. There is cruel irony in the fact that the relationships that play such a critical role in defending us from loneliness over the course of our lives are, for many, eventually lost, plunging us back into a turbulent sea of loneliness from which they once promised to save us.

'You Can't Just Sit and Look at Fish All Day, Can You?'

Peter was eighty-three years old.

'Got the mind of a twenty-five-year-old, though, that's the problem!' he bantered, as our conversation began.

He was a happy-go-lucky man, with a warm and cheerful temperament. He was keen to show me the impressive facilities in the plush, modern retirement complex where he had lived for four years, since the death of Jean, his wife. It was an appealing place and he seemed proud of the fact that the residents had their own swimming pool, gym, restaurant, cafeteria, two libraries and a games room complete with snooker table, dartboard and large-screen TV. The whole place had that plush, clean, polished feeling that high-end hotels often have. The staff even seemed like a product of the service industry, well-schooled in emotional labour. The whole place was a grandiose reflection of the hospitality-meets-retirement-living phenomenon that is taking off in the UK, for those who can afford it.

People smiled at me and were on first-name terms with Peter as he guided me around on our tour. He waved at a group of residents behind a polished glass screen; they were taking a Zumba class led by an instructor, and some of the older women waved back and sort of giggled as though they were flattered to have been recognized and acknowledged by him. He high-fived a couple of older men sitting at a polished mahogany table, playing mah-jong, and I got the impression that he was a bit of a kingpin around here.

When we reached one of the libraries, Peter decided that we ought to begin our conversation in the privacy of his apartment, so we walked along the manicured streets that led to his home. It was a sunny day, and the blue sky and cheerful, whistling gardener trimming the hedgerows made it all feel rather idyllic. At least for that moment, I was seduced into feeling as though I might like to live there when I retire too.

Peter's apartment was equally plush. He had a gleaming, luxury kitchen, and everything was spacious and spotless. I suspected it must have been professionally cleaned, and I was right. The hefty monthly service charge Peter paid not only covered the use of the facilities but also a professional cleaning service. He had two very well-behaved, placid golden Labradors, both of whom were lying quietly on the living-room floor when we arrived. They didn't bother to look in our direction, but wagged their tails in synchrony a little faster, which I took to be an acknowledgement of our arrival. Peter also had a beautiful fish tank in the living room that was fascinating to look at. He told me that there were ten different species of fish in it, and we watched them swim around for a while. I have always found looking at fish hypnotic and I could have watched them in silence all day. That's how I'd ideally choose to spend my time, I thought – like those fish, very slowly and seemingly randomly floating around in space, with no particular objective, pressure, or responsibility.

Peter hadn't had it easy, in relation to the loss of his wife. 'We'd been married for fifty-eight years when she died,' he told me, as we sat in a pair of comfortable, soft-to-the-touch, rose-coloured armchairs. 'We didn't quite make sixty years – but, yes. Yes. I was a carer for her, you know. She had Parkinson's disease. We realized that she had it about six years before she died. She had heart problems as well, and then unfortunately she died of cancer of the bowel and liver. She didn't want to go to hospital, so I cared for her for nine months while she died.'

He sighed as we both quietly contemplated what he had said.

'Then it was just me and the dogs and the fish,' he said, as though this was something to which he had resigned himself.

Peter and Jean had been together for so long that it was not particularly surprising to learn that they met at school.

'Yes. We were at school together, grammar school,' he explained. 'They put me in set B4, so obviously I wasn't very good. My wife was in A4, because she was obviously clever. However, I was transferred up to the A stream the following year and that's when I met her. I found she was the only girl I could talk to,' he paused 'We went to the pictures two or three times. I left to do this apprenticeship and education thing, and she stayed on in sixth form, went to university, and we met up again having been two years apart. That was the start of the fairy tale.' He smiled.

Sixty years later, Peter was sitting beside Jean, stroking her hair, as she drew her last breath.

'We had just bought her this orthopaedic bed that went up and down and round and round,' he told me. 'She was in that bed for the last week of her life, and all of these care people were coming in and out of our house. She didn't like it because, by that time, she was a bit incontinent.'

He paused for what felt like a long time and one of the dogs sighed into the silence.

'Where am I getting to?' he continued. 'Yes. During the last week, she was going downhill, although I didn't see it. But the doctor could see it when he came round, and the hospice care people could see it – they knew.

'Nobody has ever died in my presence before,' he continued. 'I've seen my grandparents dead, I've seen my parents dead, but nobody has actually died in front of me. She just . . . stopped breathing. I didn't know what to do. I got on the phone to Felicity, my granddaughter, and I said, "Your grandma has stopped breathing. What do I do?"'

I thought about what Mum had told me about Grandpa's death. He died in one of forty-two single rooms, with en-suite facilities, at the Vera James Care Home in Ely. Vera James is a purpose-built residential home designed to support older people living with dementia and other related illnesses. He was ninety-one. The room in which he died felt rather clinical, even though, when he'd moved in, two months earlier, he had brought with him a small, round, wooden table that he had made himself, an armchair and some pictures.

Mum told me that he died in her arms, with several other family members gathered at his bedside. She told me that she held him as he died, while they played Irish music on his stereo. He loved that stereo. He bought it in the 1980s, when flashy graphic equalizers with lots of lights and buttons seemed to be all the rage. In happier days, it saw him through many an afternoon, sitting in his armchair, wearing a ridiculously large set of headphones and exaggeratedly 'conducting' classical music with his hands, hoping we would notice how 'cultured' he was. He didn't feel like the same person when he died. He was heavily sedated, dosed up with morphine. Mum said she clearly felt him slip away in her arms.

Mum has a remarkable capacity to remain calm and resolute when she's nursing, comforting or simply holding people who are dying. I've noted that this doesn't fit with her character in the rest of her life. She'll fall to pieces in a traffic jam, be terrified of driving on the motorway, panic about the smallest of things, and will even be rattled by the fact that the toaster hasn't been put back in its proper place. But, if you're dying, I highly recommend her. A decade before Grandpa died, I watched her calmly and lovingly hold Grandma in her arms as she writhed and foamed at the mouth on the living-room floor during the onset of the stroke that would eventually kill her. I was terrified and in a state of panic, but Mum was present and took charge of that moment in a way I had never seen her do before.

She must have gained these valuable skills in how to be caring in the face of the indignity of death during her days as an auxiliary nurse at Addenbrooke's Hospital in Cambridge. She would come back from her shifts, exhausted, telling us stories about how she'd had to lug around the hospital the oversized corpses of people she'd been talking to just yesterday. She regularly talked about the ignominy of death and dying as a common occurrence in the hospital. It makes sense that she evolved so that she could just show up emotionally in the face of death. So, Grandpa was in good hands.

The death certificate attributed his death to Lewy body dementia, a progressive form of dementia thought to result from build-up of protein deposits in the nerve cells of the brain. In the latter stages, people lose the ability to care for themselves, or communicate, and dysphagia – difficulty swallowing – is not uncommon. These latter stages had prompted my grandpa – and my family – to reluctantly decide that it was in his best interests to permanently move to Vera James as his condition deteriorated. As it turned out, he lived only eight weeks longer in the care home.

Some months before he died, Grandpa's dysphagia worsened. Mum told me that she distinctly remembers his very last excursion out of the house. She took him for a drive to a local pub, hoping that he might find a fragment of enjoyment from half a pint of John Smith's Extra Smooth bitter. Though he was never much of a drinker, I distinctly remember that my grandparents kept cans of John Smith's Extra Smooth in the kitchen, at room temperature, next to the biscuit tin. They were a special treat, a reward after a hard day's work in the garden, or for when he felt like a half of bitter with lunch. In the pub that day, Mum told me that he coughed, spluttered and struggled as the warm bitter poured out of his nose and into his lap. As they drove home, he told her with sincerity that death was coming.

I am always moved, frequently to tears, by the fact that Grandpa's very last excursion was not the life-affirming embrace with one of life's pleasures that my mum had intended. Paradoxically, it seemed to confirm the opposite: that Grandpa could no longer reap even the smallest of pleasures from the world around him. Instead, like watching grains of sand slipping through his fingers, his last excursion confirmed that one of the few remaining threads of positive connection to the outside world had faded away. Grandpa's world was disintegrating, and he had an acute sense that his journey was coming to an end.

Peter had tried hard not to be completely pulled under by his own grief and loneliness, even though he knew these feelings were there, lurking, never too far away.

'I can never forget how much I miss her,' he told me. 'On her birthday and on our wedding day, for example, I deliberately don't see anyone, including the family. They just know to leave me alone. I go for a walk with the dogs, and I look at photographs. I've got lots of past photographs.'

He looked down at the dogs. One of them was lying with

her head on his slipper. 'Yes, I know, you are on some of the photographs, aren't you?' He spoke in one of those voices people use to purposely exaggerate affection while addressing animals or small children, and the dog's tail wagged lazily in acknowledgement.

To some extent, the dogs helped Peter maintain a sense of connection to his life with Jean, because they were a part of that life too, and the photographs evidenced the fact that they were a family. 'I shall be very unhappy when these dogs start dying too,' he told me. 'Hey? Won't I? When you go?' He used the voice again to address the dog at his feet.

'She's eight now, and the other one is thirteen and has noticeably slowed down during the last year,' he continued. 'My life revolves around the dogs. They've got to have their walks each day. They've got to be fed each day. They are good company. They are my girlfriends, really. And I really don't know what I'm going to do without them. That's going to be a very, very difficult time for me. You can't just sit and look at fish all day, can you?' he reasoned.

I couldn't agree – looking at fish all day sounded wonderful to me – but I kept my thoughts to myself.

Peter tried to explain the loneliness he had experienced since Jean's death by offering me a few examples. A large part of it connected to the loss and subsequent absence of physical intimacy and contact. Peter and Jean had what he called 'a little ritual' of kissing goodnight.

'My mother always told me to make sure, when you're married, to share a kiss every night, regardless of the mood you are in – because it helps no end with sleeping, and you always wake up in a better mood,' he explained. 'When my wife died and we had the funeral, I gave a little talk. I remember what I said. I said, "I'll mention this, kissing goodnight. The one thing I will miss is a goodnight kiss."'

For Peter, there was something deeply reassuring about the nightly kisses he shared with Jean. They provided regular physical confirmation that he was not alone in the world. For Peter, sharing sixty years of nightly kisses with Jean had provided him with an experience of connection that transcended words, and he missed it deeply.

Peter paused for a moment, as though he was deliberating whether to proceed with what he was about to say. I could sense that it was something he felt was a little risky, but he went for it anyway.

'I'm surprised you haven't asked me about sex yet,' he eventually said, looking at me as though my reaction mattered more than it had done up to this point in the conversation.

I told him that I'd be happy for us to talk about sex, if he felt that it was something he would like to discuss.

'Well,' he continued, clearly relieved that the risk had paid off, 'I miss it so much. It has been a huge hole in my life, since Jean died, that has been difficult to fill, especially at my age.'

Peter was a living, breathing example of the fact that physical contact, touch and intimacy are sought and necessary at all stages of the human lifespan. However, a profound and wholly ignored source of suffering in older people is the loss of physical and emotional intimacy that can so often accompany widowhood, declining health or institutionalization. The psychotherapist, Gretta Keene, has noted that, in old age, a culture of shame, lack of opportunity and even punishment can cause sexual aliveness to wither in the latter stages of life.[4] She noted how her ninety-four-year-old grandmother was reprimanded in her nursing home, 'caught' with her hands down the pants of her 'lover'.

My mind was transported back to what my grandpa had

told me that night in front of the fire, about how he could count the number of times he'd had sex with my grandma on two hands, and I'd, for the first time, considered how lonely his unsatisfied sexual desire must have been for him. I was pleased that Peter wanted to discuss the issue with me.

After a pause, he said, 'I suppose, all my life, with Jean, sex had been lovemaking. I mean, we are really getting personal now, but, when she died, I missed that so, so much.'

He tried to explain why, in his opinion, sex, or lovemaking, had become more enjoyable in old age. 'It's much, much more enjoyable in old age, you know, because, I mean, if I said it to you, you'd think, Oh, good grief, that horrible old body, all the spots and bumps and cuts and wounds, and . . . takes off a wooden leg and . . . takes out the eye. Sorry . . .'

He had clearly amused himself and he burst out laughing. His laughter was infectious, and I found myself chuckling along with him. The dogs seemed to wonder what on earth we found so amusing.

'But it's not anything like that,' he continued, 'because you both know you are in the same boat . . . You get round it, in some peculiar way, you accept it all, and the sex is wonderful.'

For Peter, withering away sexually wasn't something he was willing to tolerate. He was not the sort of man to allow his need for physical and emotional intimacy to remain unfulfilled for the rest of his life. 'There's this lady,' he told me. 'I can't kiss Jean goodnight any longer, so, this lady and I, we say goodnight with a kiss in a text every night. Yes, she's a nice lively soul, and she comes up and spends the day here every so often.'

I asked Peter her name, but he preferred not to tell me. 'I'll leave her name out. A lady from Devon,' he replied. 'I'll call her my Devonian maiden. She was born and bred – made in Devon, she was! Yes! So, she comes to visit, we pop into bed for half an hour or forty-five minutes, depending on my staying power, I make us a meal and she goes home.' He laughed.

I asked him whether he felt that he loved his Devonian maiden.

'Yes. But I wouldn't like to be married to her and I know she wouldn't like to be married to me. I think that's because I'm ten years older than her,' he replied. 'But we have a laugh.'

As it turned out, Peter had a second lover.

'You see, there's also another lady . . . In fact, she walked past here a little while ago, taking her dog for a walk.' He gestured towards the window. 'She's called April, she's a year younger than me, but we have a good laugh too. You can say almost anything you like to her and she'll either laugh or come back at you with something equally as naughty or out of this world . . . Quite often, on a Thursday, she'll say, "Come out for lunch?" So, we go and have lunch in the restaurant, we say ridiculous things to each other that I wouldn't say to other ladies.'

I asked him what he meant.

'Well, I'll say to her, "It's a bit chilly today, shall we go and have a cuddle?" And she'll say, "Oh, yes, please!" And then we both go and fully, well, you know . . .'

I knew what he meant.

I asked Peter whether he felt that his lovers were emotional confidantes as well as physical-intimacy partners.

'Hmmm. Do I confide in them about my feelings?' he reflected. 'Not nearly as much as I have to you. I've confided more to you today than anybody ever.'

Pleased that we had broached the subject of sex, Peter told

me a touching story about how Jean's death had created other
unforeseen challenges for him.

'You wouldn't think it when you talk to me,' he began, 'but
I have found it so, so hard to do the little things on my own.'

I asked him what he meant by 'the little things' and he
explained by way of a recent example.

'Well, Jean was always my mother figure when it came to
the little things in life, like buying clothes and choosing what
to wear. She "had my back" in relation to those little things
and I have been lost without her.'

Peter told me that he couldn't show me, but the underpants he was currently wearing were the product of a
challenge he'd set himself.

'I thought, I'm going to be brave, here. I shall go and get
some flash underpants. So, I got on the bus and I went into
Next. I'd seen them on the internet. I mean, the poor girl in
the shop was embarrassed because I was sort of wandering
around, looking at these pants, feeling a bit nervous and lost,'
he told me. 'I was sort of holding them up, in the way Jean
used to do when we bought my clothes. I finally got some
with purple spots on, and yellow spots, and different coloured spots. I thought, There you are! I've accomplished my
mission to brighten myself up.' He seemed genuinely proud
of himself. 'Nobody else will know, unless I have an
accident – but I can't tell you how difficult it was for me to do
that without Jean,' he concluded.

The void in Peter's life that had emerged in the aftermath
of Jean's death was connected to a myriad of these little
losses – like her presence when buying underpants – that
each contributed to an overall sense that he had lost someone
who helped him feel less alone in the world.

It is claimed that bereavement is one of the most common
causes of loneliness in older people. The Loneliness Project

reinforced what many studies of bereaved older people have found – that an acute sense of loneliness is experienced by almost all widows and widowers. If you listen carefully, it is possible to appreciate the wide range of secondary losses that, taken together, can contribute to the overall sense of loneliness that inevitably follows. It is not only the fact that we lose our husbands, wives, companions, friends and confidantes – but also that, in losing them, we risk no longer perceiving *ourselves* as husbands, wives, companions, friends or confidantes. We lose a part of ourselves and a part of our identity that often challenges us to engage in a painful redefinition of self. That's how I imagined Peter felt.

The Star in the Distance (Right Ascension 19h 27m 53.83s, Declination 42° 58' 19.94")

It's 1983. I am four years old. My family are gathered in the living room of our cottage in rural Cambridgeshire – Cobbler's Cottage. Mum is sitting on the pale green sofa my grandparents donated to us when they updated their three-piece suite to something slightly more luxurious. The walls are papered so that the top half of the room is covered in a 'country floral' design, chosen by Mum, and the bottom half in a two-tone, green-striped design, chosen by Dad. The two halves are separated by a varnished wooden dado rail. The room is decorated this way as a compromise because my parents can't agree on a wallpaper pattern. The different wallpaper patterns are something I never feel work all that well together, and they are a constant reminder of the fact that my parents don't either.

Dad is sitting on a dining chair he has positioned next to the sofa, wearing a checked shirt and blue bell-bottom jeans. He is playing his guitar. Dad is a serious guitarist and his claim to fame is that his band, Cat-Squirrel, was once the warm-up for Status Quo and other major acts. My brother is about three years old, and my sister is even younger. We are dancing in the living room while Dad plays a succession of campfire and soft-rock songs. I am finding it fun, and I am happy. The happiness moves me to experiment with my dance moves – marching, jumping, hopping, fooling around with my brother and sister. I feel a warm sense of belonging in my body, a fuzzy four-year-old feeling of familial love. We are sharing something joyous, and I am, for that moment in time, suspended in a state of happiness.

Suddenly, I feel a powerful sense of love towards Dad, as if the general sense of love in my body abruptly transforms into something concentrated, directed solely at him. I look at his handsome face and strong torso and admire how he – with the help of his guitar – is the orchestrator of this joyful moment in my little life. I feel a sudden urge to be close to him and I instinctively act upon it in an uninhibited, carefree way – something I will, over time, evolve not to do when I feel a powerful surge of love towards someone, for fear of being rejected, shut down or humiliated if it isn't reciprocated. I will become a more cautious, conservative creature when it comes to the expression of love, but it wasn't always like that. I run to Dad's lap, hop on and snuggle into him, genuinely expecting to be welcomed, held and lovingly received.

I'm not sure if he is consciously aware of it, but his response to my expression of love is incongruent. He seems almost insulted by what I have done, and assertively, yet not aggressively, pushes me off his lap. Some people are deeply uncomfortable when others express love towards them, and it can, for a variety of reasons, elicit a powerful set of emotional responses, such as anger, discomfort, shame, frustration, fear or anxiety. Dad seems angry, offended, uncomfortable – all of the above – and it's clear that he wants me off his lap ASAP. Perhaps he is simply annoyed and frustrated that I have jumped into his lap while he is trying to concentrate on playing his guitar. Maybe it is more deep-rooted than that.

Maybe the moment was insignificant to Dad. I doubt whether he even remembered it afterwards. But I will remember it for as long as I live. In the literature on attachment, there's a phenomenon that psychologists have called an 'attachment wound'. The technical way of explaining it is as a perceived rejection, abandonment, betrayal or breach of trust at a critical moment of need, by someone you expected to be there for you. These attachment wounds can feel traumatic and can turn out to be pivotal moments in the development – or not – of closeness in relationships. What happened with Dad that day in 1983 felt traumatic for me – even if it was only trauma with a small *t* – and I think it inflicted an early attachment wound.

It really stings and I stagger off his lap under the force of his shove. I turn and walk away, like a punch-drunk boxer who has taken a serious blow to the head. It makes it worse that I can hear Mum's voice in the background, providing a running commentary of my experience of shame and rejection. 'Les?! What are you doing?!' she exclaims incredulously. 'He came to you for a cuddle, and you just pushed him away?' Dad coldly tells her to 'shush' and continues playing his guitar. Meanwhile, I am privately drowning in a turbulent sea of shame, embarrassment, rejection and abandonment.

It is one of my first experiences of how lonely it can feel to look for a sense of emotional closeness and intimacy from someone you are willing to trust, to openly express your love and vulnerability, to 'show them your cards' in an emotional sense, but be rejected by them all the same.

I don't know why I don't cry, because I cry if I cut my knee or have a fight with my brother or sister. Perhaps I am in that emotionally numb place where you simply *can't* cry, *can't* respond, and you are floating in a state of disbelief. I think there is probably a bit of 'Well, fuck you' in it too. I don't want to show him that he has hurt me, that I am weak, that I need him, that I love him. I feel angry and betrayed. Inside, my undeveloped psyche is already scrabbling around trying to adapt to what amounts to a significant emotional body blow.

It's 2022. Years of soul searching, and not-insignificant amounts of psychotherapy, have led me to conclude that what happened in the living room in 1983 was probably a critical incident that reflected the script for my relationship with Dad – a frequently lonely, barren relationship, in which I could never quite get close enough to him. The author and psychoanalyst, Clarissa Pinkola Estés, has used a desert metaphor to describe the lonely nature of some relationships.[5] I picture my relationship with Dad as though I'm walking through a sandy, dusty, flat desert landscape. I can see him in the distance, but he's very far away and there's a lot of sand blowing around, obscuring him from my view. In the image, I'm thirsty and I'd really like to ask him for a drink, but it feels too risky. I'd sooner tough it out myself than risk showing him my yearning. I have plodded and struggled on through the desert because beautiful things do grow – even in the desert. They may be few and far between, but there are unusual, often stunning species of vegetation to be found. Desert landscapes are home to the sweet fruit of the prickly pear, the blooms of the Baja fairy duster, the wonder of the cinnamon cactus and carpets of gorgeous desert flowers. It could be argued that their sparsity makes their beauty more discernible. Like desert vegetation, there will be a handful of strikingly powerful moments in my life when I get to experience Dad just as I longed to experience him as a four-year-old, that day, in 1983.

*

It's 1989. I am ten years old. I am teary, anxious, terrified and feeling deeply unsafe at the prospect of travelling away from home, alone, on a sports trip to a foreign country, with a group of children and adults I do not really know. It is one of those things that sounded like an exciting prospect when I first signed up for it, but it terrifies me with increasing intensity as the day of reckoning approaches. I'm not ready to be away from my home and family for such a long period of time, with no immediate way of getting back, and with nobody I know or trust in close proximity. I now feel strongly that I no longer want to go, but we are leaving for the airport in three hours.

Mum is angry with me for being so upset. She'd hoped it would be a joyous occasion and she'd be waving me off as I excitedly took one of my first steps towards independence. But it doesn't happen that way. My feelings of terror and reluctance intensify until I can no longer contain them. I run to the bottom of the garden, to the big apple tree, and sit on the tractor tyre that Dad strung up to the sturdiest branch. The two blue fibreglass ropes cut and splinter your hands if you grip them too tightly, but I grip them tightly anyway. I am crying uncontrollably and my vulnerability and fear have reached a peak. I am past the point of no return and the surge of emotion is simply too powerful even for my already well-developed defences to hold in. I can't tough it out or pretend I am OK.

As I sob, I suddenly realize that Dad is standing right in front of me. I open my eyes and, in an instant, he pulls me into his strong, warm body. He holds me just as I wanted him to all those years ago. He holds me tightly and speaks to me softly, instinctively comforting and soothing me in a way that only a father's embrace can. For that short moment, he is my guardian angel, my cinnamon cactus, my carpet of beautiful desert flowers. I may have walked for many years to stumble across a moment like this – but it feels well worth the effort.

I often wondered why. Why, in that moment, could he be there for me? Why couldn't that be how he loved me all the time? I had a theory. Perhaps it was the fact that every cell in my body was screaming with the sort of primal vulnerability and terror that even Dad couldn't fail to notice. Maybe that's what it took for him to recognize my need for love and protection, or to activate his inner paternal spirit. Sometimes, I blamed myself. Maybe I shot myself in the foot by becoming too good at disguising my vulnerability from him. Metaphorically speaking, I wouldn't see further desert vegetation for many more years. But I did see it, from time to time, and I had at least tasted something that could exist in my relationship with Dad in just enough abundance for me to keep trudging and hoping.

Carl Jung used the term 'father hunger' for what I'm describing. The psychoanalyst James Hollis, thinks that we all secretly long for the body, strength, wisdom and love of our father. When our yearning is frustrated, we can carry the deficit through life and it can feel like something is missing, as though our psyche is craving an essential nutrient. It's not surprising that we might look for that nutrient elsewhere, in inappropriate places, feel angry about it, or grieve its absence. There is compelling evidence from my life that I have done all of these. But, as James Hollis has also noted, 'there is no point in a man blaming his father, for his father could then blame his father. The chain of cause and effect reaches back to the beginning of industrial and urban man.'[6]

It's February 2022. It's a rainy, overcast day, and I am visiting Dad as he dies in the corner of ward D5 at Addenbrooke's

Hospital, Cambridge. The consultant has called to tell me there is nothing more they can do. He is dying of liver and kidney complications stemming from a carcinoma of the pancreas and he's slipped into an unconscious state from which he will not return. He isn't expected to last the night. As it turns out, he will hold on for five more days. The nurse who checks on him at 4.30 a.m. on Friday morning will find him dead.

The beige-coloured curtain is drawn around his bed when the nurse guides me to his cubicle. There are three other patients on the ward, but I don't pay any attention to them; my focus is sharply concentrated on the curtain that inadequately separates Dad from the rest of the room. I am terrified. I want to run away when I first see him lying there, occasionally flinching, his face slightly contorted, struggling for breath, no longer fully alive. He is yellow, which is a common consequence of the jaundice induced by the biliary obstruction associated with pancreatic cancer, and I notice how frail and emaciated his legs are, even though all but their outline is obscured from my view by the sheets. I remember how, as a child, I was always impressed with how strong and well-muscled Dad's legs were. I would walk behind him on hikes, or adventures, and take a mental note of his muscular calves. But they are now a withered shadow of their former glory. My senses are heightened to the extent that I seem to notice everything about him. I appreciate how the grey hairs of his beard grow in interesting and unusual formations, how beautifully curly his hair is, and the smoothness of the yellowed skin on his upper right arm reminds me of the honey and Moroccan argan oil conditioner I have been using.

I approach his bedside as a wounded, needy, vulnerable little child. A part of me is desperate to feel as close to him as I felt that day at the bottom of the garden in 1989, under the apple tree, when he held me. I fantasize about climbing under the sheets and just holding him, lying there, feeling close to his body in a way that has been so painfully elusive for most of my life. It takes me some time to adjust to the fact that this may be the very first time I've seen Dad so completely and utterly vulnerable. I ask for a little time on my own with him and the nurse tells me she thinks he can still hear me.

'LESLIE! LESLIE . . .' she says loudly, gently shaking his shoulder as though she is trying to wake him from a deep sleep. 'THERE'S SOMEONE HERE TO SEE YOU, LESLIE. THAT'S NICE, ISN'T IT?' She turns to me and says, in a sort of half-whisper, 'They can hear more than you think, you know.'

I have things I want to tell Dad. I want to tell him that I love him, and it feels urgent that he knows this. I want to tell him that, wherever he is going next, I hope he will find peace. I want to tell him I am grateful for the things we have managed to share and the gifts he has given me. And none of these things feel like they are platitudes – I feel like I need to tell him from the bottom of my heart.

I also feel a need to touch him as I speak to him. At first, I touch his arm, like a child prodding something mysterious they have found in a rock pool. But, as my reticence evaporates, I place the palm of my hand gently on his yellow skin, close my eyes and speak.

'I love you, Dad. And Em, and Mum, and Joe – they told me to tell you they love you too.'

At first, it feels as though what I am saying distresses us both. Dad seems to become more restless and uncomfortable, and I feel a powerful turbulence filling my body and his. But, as I continue to touch him and talk, my words transition into a general rambling about anything and everything, and the connection between us seems to soften and feel more serene.

My ex-partner, Natalie, joins me at his bedside after what feels like about twenty minutes, but may, in fact, she later tells me, have been much less time than that. She has a sort of instinctive maternal quality that immediately kicks in. She puts her hand gently on Dad's other shoulder, as I continue to touch his right arm, and she speaks to him in a soothing way about things like the weather, the view from the window next to his bed, and how she is glad to have met him (they hadn't met before that day), even if the circumstances aren't what they would have wanted. As is often the case with loving words, it doesn't really matter *what* she says – the comfort is in how it is delivered. My grandma was good at that too – she would cuddle you and talk about completely random things that didn't really matter, but it made you feel warm and loved simply because she delivered what she was saying with such affection.

We sit with Dad and gently talk to him for perhaps another twenty minutes, at which point I suddenly become aware that the dynamic has shifted. When I arrived, I felt like a wounded, vulnerable child, still yearning for the love, protection and nurturance I had always craved from him. When we leave, for the first time in my life, I appreciate the vulnerable child inside Dad too, and I am happy that we've been able to briefly meet with that part of him before he dies.

On our way out of the hospital, we stop to sit in the chapel and reflect. We are shell-shocked, emotionally drained and filled with the existentially challenging thoughts and emotions often prompted by being in death's vicinity. As we sit on the purple meeting-room chairs in the front row, staring at a wooden cross and a faux yucca plant in the corner, I picture myself sitting down in the desert that reflected my relationship with Dad. In my mind's eye, I am hugging my knees, resting my head on my forearms, as the harsh desert winds blow around me. I always felt lonely in that desert, but I cannot imagine my life without it – and, paradoxically, there is a deep sense of loneliness in the knowledge that I'll never again encounter the beautiful, yet incredibly sparse, desert vegetation.

Even in the desert of my relationship with Dad, however, there were unlikely and unexpected pools of water, the most refreshing of which I experienced a few days before he died. The last time I had a coherent conversation with him was days before he was admitted to hospital and fell unconscious. I had just come out of the supermarket and Alex was sitting in the car because he had decided, some years ago, that he hated supermarkets and now refused to accompany me inside. I had just started the car when my phone rang, the car having automatically connected it to the Bluetooth speaker system. As we drove out of the supermarket, I answered the call. It was Dad. He didn't sound completely out of it, as he often did when he called, on account of the fact that he'd been drinking, and he told me that he wanted to tell me something.

Alex and I listened through the car speaker system as he spoke.

'So, I bought one of your books on Amazon, the other day.'

'Really?' I was genuinely surprised. I'd always been pretty sure Dad didn't know what I did for a living, let alone what I'd written. So, I was a little confused. 'OK,' I said. 'Which book did you buy, Dad?'

'Ummm, that one about motivation, or something or other . . .' he replied.

He'd bought a copy of an academic monograph I'd written a couple of years back, a pretty heavy-going thesis about the ways in which the neoliberal education system is throttling human motivation. It was the sort of book you'd expect graduate students and fellow academics to read – but not Dad. He'd always preferred the light biographies of legendary heroes.

'Look,' he continued, 'I'll be honest with you, Sam, I didn't really understand it – not a word of it.' He chuckled. 'So, it must be a clever book. I just want you to know that I'm really impressed that you wrote it and I'm proud of you. I want you to remember that.'

I didn't know what to say. It was the first time he had told me that he was proud of me or shown a genuine interest in something I'd created. I can't remember a time he attended a parents' evening, or asked me about my schoolwork, or showed an interest in something I'd written. And yet, here we were. He was probably sitting in that tattered old armchair, with the TV blaring out, wearing his dressing gown, underpants and a Panama hat, with a box of cider next to him – trying to read my book in the final few days of his life.

'Thank you, Dad,' I replied. 'That really does mean a lot to me. You needn't have bought it, you know – it's massively overpriced and I could have sent you a copy.'

It's March 2022. We have started clearing out the small one-bedroom council bungalow where Dad lived, on the outskirts of Cambridge. It strikes me just how much there is to do when someone you love dies. On the one hand, there's the practical stuff, like sorting out belongings, closing bank accounts, stopping direct debits and ensuring that everyone who needs to know about the death – from the passport agency to the DVLA and the local council – is informed. Then there's the funeral arrangements, the wake, the invitations, the order of service, the food and refreshments, the cremation, and more besides. It feels like a lot to deal with, when you're simultaneously trying to cope with the emotional challenges grief presents. For a while, the practical stuff preoccupies me to the extent that I cry in the cracks between the blocks of time devoted to these practical tasks. I let my grief out while driving, doing the washing up or taking a shower.

My brother, my sister, her partner Ed, my ex-partner Natalie and I sort through the remnants of Dad's life on a drizzly Saturday afternoon in Cambridge. He didn't leave a will, so diplomatically and respectfully we each lay claim to the things we want to hold on to. Ed takes a shine to things like the sledgehammer, an old machete from the shed and an array of interesting tools. My brother chooses Dad's pride and joy, the vintage, red Gretsch Astro-Jet electric guitar from the Cat-Squirrel heydays. My sister, who is six months pregnant, takes the ukulele – Dad had told her he wanted to teach his grandson how to play – and the bench he used to sit on by the front porch. Natalie curiously takes a shine to a peculiar cheap replica of a large French railway-station clock that Dad, for some reason, adored and had presented as a feature of his living room for many years, on the wall behind his tattered old armchair.

We drive home with a strimmer, a hedge trimmer, the Panama hat Dad wore, one of his six-string acoustic guitars, a twelve-string guitar, an electric guitar, a white plastic bag filled with harmonicas, a garden hoe, a pile of audio cassettes and the old black shoulder bag he used to carry – complete with Werther's Originals, a green packet of Rizla papers, a map of Germany and a box of Cat-Squirrel business cards. These objects are all I have to connect me to Dad; he was the only man in my life I've ever wanted to be truly close to, but we could never quite manage it. I cry that night, surrounded by the curious set of artefacts that I pray will somehow compensate for the fact that any remote hopes I had of feeling that elusive sense of connection to Dad have probably died with him.

Since his death, there are certain photographs of Dad that, for some reason, are exceptionally painful for me to look at – they all depict him in his twenties or early thirties. There's a picture of him standing at the open door of an old, light blue 1970s Mini. He's leaning on the door of the car, the sun is shining, and there are flat, expansive, open fields of wheat and barley behind him. He looks tanned and he's smiling so that his eyes light up and twinkle deeply. He's fully alive. He's wearing a tight red T-shirt and a pair of black trousers. It's one of those photographs that captures genuine happiness and contentment, rather than the sort that has clearly been contrived or orchestrated. Dad looks like the epitome of strength and youthfulness.

At first, I don't really understand why this photograph would provoke a more powerful emotional reaction in me than, say, photographs of Dad in his childhood, or of us together during his midlife or later years. It suddenly dawns on me when I am driving back from the funeral, listening to an old recording of Cat-Squirrel covering 'Badge' (a hit for Cream in 1969), with my dad on vocals, that the 'Dad' in that picture is the closest reflection of the version of 'Dad' I had idolized all those years ago in the living room, as a four-year-old, or in the garden, under the apple tree. As I look at those photographs, the small child that's still inside me somewhere blatant dishonesty and his lack of capacity to respect her wishes on the matter seemed to inflame and ignite her anger. In turn, her tendency to verbally insult and demean him when she was angry ignited and inflamed *his* anger. His dinner was typically overcooked, dry and almost inedible by the time he got home, and Mum would either give it to the dog, in anger, or throw it on the table in front of him. Over the years, it felt as though the meals she prepared for him reflected her loss of respect for him. Roast dinners and lasagnes were gradually replaced by tinned faggots, burned sausages, potato waffles and the charred remains of a Findus Crispy Pancake or two.

The anger, resentment, fear and pain swirled around and created an atmosphere that filled the house like thick, black, toxic smoke. As Dad sat down to eat his dinner, you could hear his jaw crunching and cracking as he chewed, probably a consequence of his malocclusion or temporomandibular disorder, which caused things to clunk every time he opened and closed his mouth. You just knew that everything about him – his presence, the way he ate, the way he sat, the way he breathed – was fuelling and stirring the cauldron of intense resentment Mum felt towards him. The arguments would ignite, die down and then reignite periodically over the course of the evening, often becoming more animated and vocal after we children had gone to bed. Mum usually slept alone in their bedroom with Max, our black-and-white Welsh springer spaniel, and I'd often hear her crying before she went to sleep following an argument. Dad pretty much always slept on the couch. I could hear him preparing extravagant midnight snacks and watching episodes of *Sergeant Bilko* into the early hours of the morning. Over time, he got tired of the couch, and he used to dig out the camp bed from the cupboard under the stairs and place it on the experiences a profound sensation of grief at the loss of the body, strength, vitality and protection of his father.

It's late March 2022, a few days after Dad's funeral. I am sitting alone at my desk on a rainy Wednesday morning, and I register a star in Dad's name. I don't tell anybody that I plan to do it – it just happens impulsively. I pay about forty pounds for the privilege of naming an extra bright star in the Lyra constellation of the northern sky after Dad. I select the Lyra constellation because it has a mythological connection to music. Apparently, it represents the lyre – a stringed instrument used in antiquity – and is associated with the myth of the Greek musician and poet Orpheus. It was first catalogued by the astronomer Ptolemy in the second century. Dad's star, which I unimaginatively name 'Leslie James Carr', can be found slightly to the left of Vega, the brightest star in the Lyra constellation, at the following coordinates: right ascension 19h 27m 53.83s, declination 42° 58′ 19.94″. I make sure that I can find it on a Digital Sky Survey optical image. I realize I have no chance of spotting it with any precision when I'm gazing up at the night sky, but at least I'll have a rough idea of where it is. It's such a long way away, but I take comfort from the fact that Dad is now somewhere out there, in the distance – just as he has always been.

Paradoxically, relationships can be a part of the problem *and* the solution, when it comes to loneliness. It is lonely when you've never managed to find closeness, intimacy or warmth with a fellow human being. It is also lonely when you pin your hopes on someone you trusted to provide closeness, intimacy and warmth, only to find that they are unwilling or unable to provide it. And it can feel lonely when we are lucky enough to find closeness, intimacy and warmth, only to have it snatched away.

But it is heartening to witness the ways in which life so often seems to reconfigure itself, offering shafts of light or rays of hope when it seems as though there's no way out. I once had a brief obsession with a TV docuseries called *I Shouldn't Be Alive*, which ran from 2005 to 2012 and featured accounts of individuals or groups caught in life-threatening scenarios in natural environments. In one episode, a man was forced to abandon his plane, parachuting into the vast expanse of open ocean below. He survived, floating in the ocean for many days before eventually washing up on a small island. I have always been simultaneously fascinated and ter-rified by the idea of being alone in the ocean, and his story captivated me. In one part, he described a moment on his second night alone in the sea, when darkness began to des-cend and the terror of being alone in the ocean intensified. As he drifted, increasingly exhausted, without a flotation device, hundreds of miles from land and losing all hope, he noticed something coming towards him through the water: a dark, sinister shape that he irrationally decided was a croco-dile. In his mind, he prepared for death, but, as the shape moved close enough for him to touch, he realized that it was a large tree trunk, just drifting around in the open ocean. The dead tree saved his life. He draped his body over its cold, slip-pery surface and survived his ordeal thanks in large part to the sanctuary it provided.

The man attributed his luck to a miracle. And it is miracu-lous how shoots of hope find their way into the darkest of places, through the tiniest of cracks, like that 'little thrill' of independence and freedom Paula told me about after the agony of Bob's death. Jake stumbled upon the same sort of thing with Zak. And, in his Devonian maiden, Peter seemed to find some sort of resolution for at least a part of the predicament in which he found himself after losing Jean. Perhaps their stories provide some evidence that life has a propensity to reconfigure these things, although I recognize this could be wishful thinking on my part, and that, for every person adrift in the ocean – metaphorically as well as literally – there may be tens, hundreds, even thousands of people who perish alone in the open sea.

PART TWO

INVISIBILITY

The Surprising Benefits of a Boring Packed Lunch

I knew from the moment you were born that I would never love anyone as much as I love you. They sent me home from the hospital shortly after you arrived on 15 September 2008, at 11.58 a.m. I was exhausted because we'd been there since 9.30 p.m. the previous evening and I hadn't slept a wink. Before they sent me home, they wrapped you in a blanket, dressed you in a tiny cream-coloured hat and allowed me to feed you your first bottle. I held you and, while you were glugging a bottle of formula, we looked into each other's eyes for the first time. As I sat at home alone that evening, I wept before I could sleep. Something inside me knew that the most significant relationship in my life had arrived and that things would never be the same again. My tears reflected joy, fear and terror, as my psyche scrabbled around, wrestling with the fact that I was now at least partially responsible for how your childhood would pan out. I was suddenly painfully and acutely aware that I didn't want you to grow up in the barren desert landscape I had shared with Dad.

I saw a little boy in my dreams that night. At first, I couldn't see his face; he was running around, playing happily in the garden. I immediately recognized it as the garden at Cobbler's Cottage. There were distinguishing features, like the football goal Dad built and painted bright blue, the sandpit, the climbing frame, the tyres that hung from the branches of the large apple tree, the summer house, the compost heap, and the wild, overgrown blackberry bushes that separated our garden from the endless arable land beyond. In my dream, I was so sure the little boy was you. I was watching you play as an invisible presence with a bird's eye view of everything. I was crying because I didn't want you to feel the sort of pain I had experienced in that sparse, barren, empty paternal landscape I shared with Dad. I wanted to protect you from that sort of loneliness and pain. I wanted to spare you from that childhood desert. At the end of the dream, the little boy suddenly stopped playing and turned around so that I could see his face. He looked up and I saw that it was me. For me, parenthood started with a powerful recognition in my soul that I didn't want you to suffer what I had found so incredibly hard to endure.

I know that it's naive to think that your parents can protect you from the inevitabilities of being human. I know that my spiritual quest to shield you from my paternal fate does not insure you against your own demons. You were three years old the night your mum left. I looked at you, sleeping the uniquely peaceful sleep of a tiny child who doesn't yet understand that the world eventually comes for us all with knives out. I gently stroked your hair and tried to fight the feelings of guilt and sadness, struggling with an overwhelming need to protect you from the undeniable fact that, while you slept, we had changed the way your family operated. Around me, the TV, the bed, the armchair and various items of furniture and decor were gone. It felt like half of our world had been stripped away.

You know those long drives we used to take some evenings when you were little? The ones I used to call 'midnight drives' to make them sound more exciting and adventurous for you, even though it was typically only around 7.30 p.m.? You would sit in the front seat, ready for bed, in a tiny pair of Angry Birds pyjamas and your pale blue Gruffalo dressing gown. I know how much you loved those drives. We used to say that it felt as though we were in a spaceship, alone together in the blackness, just seeing where the journey took us. The social-work professor, Harry Ferguson, has written about the unique space that car journeys offer for communication and therapeutic connection.[1] The car, he argues, can be a space that embodies freedom and exploration, away from the constraints of day-to-day life. I remember how much you liked to talk and share on our 'midnight drives'. We once talked about how, metaphorically speaking, our relationship is more of an island than a desert.

The other day, we were sitting at the dining table after dinner, on a typical Thursday night. Alex was doing his homework and I was working on some draft chapters of this book. Our cat, Percy, was pacing around behind us, miaowing and making his presence felt in the hope that I'd open another pouch of Whiskas in gravy. As we usually do, we chatted, joked and shared some of the details of what we were each working on. Alex's task, for his Year 8 art class, was to draw a Gaudí-inspired representation of a tower, which, for some reason, also had to incorporate the geometry and colour scheme of fruit. The base of his tower was inspired by the dragon fruit and the top morphed into a pineapple-like structure. It was an impressive creation, and I could tell that he was, for once, quite pleased with what he had produced.

As he was adding the colour to his tower, he asked me to read him something I'd written. So, while he finished shading the pink and green dragon-fruit-inspired lower structures of his tower, I read him a draft of 'The Star in the Distance'. I chose this chapter because I felt that he might connect with the fact that it was a story about his family. He listened attentively and was clearly engaged. Only once was the silence broken, because he dropped his pencil and politely apologized. When I'd finished reading, there was a silent pause as we both reflected. I wondered how he would respond. Eventually, he found the words he wanted.

'So, is your book essentially saying that everyone's lonely, in one way or another?' he asked astutely. 'Are these all just different ways that people can *be* lonely?'

I was taken aback by the clarity in his summation. 'Yeah, that's exactly it,' I said. 'That's a great way to put it, Alex.'

He looked at me and prepared to say something that I could sense felt a little bit risky for him. 'Then why don't you write about me too?' he continued. 'I'm lonely too, you know, and I'd like to tell you about how it's hard for me to show the world who I am.'

In that moment, I experienced emotional conflict. On the one hand, I was proud of his capacity to recognize something like loneliness as an inevitable and infinite part of every human life, including his own. On the other, I felt a jarring sense of guilt and failure that connected to my own unrealistic desire to shield him from the pitfalls of being human.

Ever since he was tiny, Alex and I have taken our annual road trip to visit my mum, sister and brother on the other side of the country. On our most recent trip, as we set off on the five-hour drive to Cambridge, we agreed we'd use some of the journey time to explore his experiences of loneliness. The car felt like a fitting place for us to talk more about them.

'I felt it when you were reading me the stories that night,' he told me, as we battled the endless roundabouts that constitute the outskirts of Milton Keynes. 'I could feel myself wanting to tell you about my own feelings of loneliness, but

I also had the feeling that nobody would find my story interesting or want to hear it. So, it was hard for me to actually suggest that you could write about me. I don't usually put myself forward like that. I don't think people would want to know about me.'

'But, nonetheless, you *did* suggest it. Isn't that why we're having this conversation?' I ventured.

'Yes,' he agreed. 'But I was fighting something inside me to say that.'

And so, we talked about the fact that Alex doesn't really feel people would want to hear about who he is.

'I mean, when I have the opportunity to connect to people, I won't let them see me or know me, because I'm worried about what they might think of me,' he reflected.

I asked him if he could remember when he started to feel that way.

'You know,' he answered, 'when I was little, I was the exact opposite. I could say whatever I liked, and I didn't care what people thought of me or whether they liked me. I don't know where it all started. But it did. I'm scared that people won't like me if I show them who I am.'

'OK, so, how does that connect to your feelings of *loneliness*?' I asked him.

'Because nobody really knows me. Nobody really knows who I am,' he answered. 'That's a bit lonely, isn't it? There are so many opportunities where I could share things about myself, but I don't because I don't think they'd want to know.'

He offered me a recent example from school.

'Once, at school, in IT, we had this teacher and she set this thing to do. You had to say what kind of music you liked, put it on a PowerPoint presentation, your favourite band or artist, and explain why you liked it,' he recalled. 'It was so hard for me to actually say what I liked that I told her I never listened to music. I lied to her so that I didn't have to say what I liked. She ended up telling me what *she* liked, and I put that on my PowerPoint and didn't have to reveal anything about myself.'

I asked him if he knew, at the time, what his favourite sort of music was.

'Of course, I knew,' he replied definitively. 'I like stuff, lots of stuff, but I just couldn't risk telling people because I was so afraid of being judged.'

He told me that he sometimes pretends that his preferences, likes or opinions are the same as other people's, or the same as the most prevalent opinion, so that he can more easily blend into the crowd. In primary school, he would request the most boring packed lunches he could possibly imagine – a plain digestive biscuit, a couple of dry crackers and a 'boring piece of fruit, like a banana'. Crisps, chocolate bars or anything deemed to be exciting – like, perhaps, a chicken leg, cold sausage or chocolate muffin – were 'out of the question'. His aim, he explained, was to ensure that nobody would notice him, and that the dull, tedious lunch would somehow help him melt into the background.

'It doesn't always work, though,' he reflected. 'In the end, my IT class were all flabbergasted that I didn't listen to music, and I looked like the biggest weirdo in the world because I was the only person who didn't have a favourite band! It backfired and my attempt to keep myself out of the spotlight sort of inadvertently thrust me into it.'

We talked about how it made him feel to hide himself from others in the way he was describing.

'Well, I'd like to be better friends with a lot of people,' he told me. 'And I know that this sort of gets in the way of that. But I'm not sure how to get round it. I've been making more of an effort to show people who I am lately. I'm trying because I don't want it to be that way for the rest of my life.'

He didn't seem upset or panicked by what he was telling me. In fact, he spoke in a calm, collected, unruffled manner, a bit like a surgeon talking you through open-heart surgery as though it's no big deal. I admired the fact that, at such a young age, he wasn't worrying about these internal dilemmas, but could appreciate and accept them for what they were, and had the capacity to articulate them so eloquently.

I want you to know that I have reflected on what you told me about yourself, about your loneliness. I won't lie to you. At first, I was panicked by the fact that you might have to encounter loneliness too. That's partly because I love you and there's something about the idea of you struggling with loneliness that hurts me. It's also partly because I thought it might be my fault, that any sort of suffering you encounter automatically reflects parental weakness or failure on my part. But, on reflection, I don't think it's particularly uncommon to be afraid to show the world who you are, for a myriad of complex and very human reasons. Maybe you would find it comforting to know that, like you, I also find it hard to show the world who I am. I've developed quite different mechanisms and techniques to help me 'blend in' and 'hide', but I do understand where you're coming from. Perhaps you'll find it comforting to know that I feel that way too. And so do many other people.

I'll give you an example. It became apparent very early in my life that I would be a good listener. When I was five years old, we were stuck in endless traffic on the M25, in Mum's blue Lada Samara, on the way to visit Grandma and Grandpa. My brother and sister were very small and were sitting in the back of the car; Mum was driving and I sat in the front seat. I remember that it was an extremely hot day and our car overheated. It was one of those tropical summers in the UK, when all the road surfaces soften and become malleable because of the viscoelasticity of the tarmac. There was steam coming from underneath the bonnet, a faint smell of burning, and Mum was beside herself with panic. She was crying and fretting, and something inside me knew that I had to take control of the situation. On that journey, I became a sort of five-year-old psychotherapist. I soothed Mum's anxiety, I absorbed her heightened emotion, and I listened non-judgementally to her worries, concerns and internal dialogue.

We made it to Grandma and Grandpa's house. As it turned out, the radiator cap wasn't screwed on properly and Grandpa quickly remedied the problem. I was lauded for my calm, composed, empathic listening skills. They said that I had 'saved' Mum and that, if it wasn't for me, 'who knows what would have happened?' I felt a great sense of pride and that my value and worth increased exponentially as my identity as a listener began to crystallize. I never really looked back. I'm not sure if it was written in the stars, whether I was moulded by the fact that I was always surrounded by people who desperately needed a listener, or whether I subconsciously sought out such people.

Now, I'm such a good listener that people who have a burning desire to be listened to can pretty much sniff me out. If I go to a wedding, party or social gathering, the 'unlistened-to' are attracted to me like bees to a honeypot. They find me, they talk, and I listen. I'm not pretending to listen, either. I give them my full, undivided attention. I'm empathic, compassionate, and I know how to help them feel like they have been truly heard. My point is that I'm more comfortable listening because, when I'm listening, it doesn't have to be about me. Just like you, when you try to blend in and become invisible by pretending you share the view of the majority or have nothing to offer but a dry digestive and a boring banana for lunch, I have found that I can make myself invisible by taking on the role of the listener. As the listener, I'm often just a faceless screen upon which people project themselves and have their existence corroborated for a while. Don't get me wrong, there is great reward in being the listener, but it's also a tool through which I too have been able to avoid the risk of being seen in the world.

It was the comedian Jim Carrey who said that, 'Your need for acceptance can make you invisible in this world. Risk being seen in all of your glory.' I hope that one day you too feel ready to take the risk to reveal a little more of yourself to the world. And, when you do, perhaps I will be around to reflect on it with you – on a 'midnight drive' somewhere in the future.

'With Mother Teresa, Down in the Slums'

From the beginning, I was struck by June's immaculate, orderly appearance. Her grey hair was neatly tied up in a bun on the top of her head, she had a noticeably kind face, and she spoke softly and politely, with a well-to-do accent. I immediately got the impression that she didn't have an aggressive bone in her body. She was one of those subservient people who are deeply apologetic about things they have no reason to be apologetic about.

'I'm so sorry you found it so hard to find us,' she said contritely, on my arrival. 'I really, really am; I should have given you better instructions. Anyway, do come in, young man, and I'll ask Roger to make you some coffee.'

Roger was June's husband, and I sensed that he had been waiting to determine whether it was safe to leave June in the house with me before he went about his business. He had just finished tying the laces on his shiny brown leather brogues, and he had his hat, coat and scarf on, as though he was ready to go out. Like June, he was polite, and he shook my hand warmly and followed up on the offer of a cup of coffee.

While Roger went out to the kitchen, June took me through to the sitting room. I sat on a large, expensive-looking floral-patterned sofa, and June sat opposite me in an equally expensive-looking armchair. There was something regal about her, like a monarch posing for a portrait. Their home was decadent and luxurious, and I sensed that money had never been an issue for them. June and Roger were in their late seventies and had moved into their current home a few years ago to be closer to their children, after a lifetime spent travelling the globe for Roger's career in banking.

When Roger brought my coffee on a tray, with the cafetière, milk jug and sugar bowl neatly arranged alongside a small plate of shortbread and a silver spoon, I thanked him. He seemed satisfied that I wasn't a threat, and told us he'd see us again in a few hours. We heard him close the front door and drive away in their Mercedes C-Class Coupé, and June began to tell me her story.

She was the daughter of a foreign ambassador and had spent much of her childhood – and her life – travelling the world in accordance with where her father, and later her husband, had been posted.

'I left boarding school in Australia aged eighteen,' she remembered, 'and then I stayed on in Sydney and did a one-year secretarial course. At that stage in my life, my father suddenly got posted as the ambassador to Japan. So, he came in one night and simply said, "We're moving to Japan," and I said, "I'm not going with you," and my sister said, "I'm not going either." But he said, "Girls, I'm not asking you. I am *telling* you – you are *going* to Japan with me." We could tell by the tone of his voice that it wasn't up for debate.'

She paused and looked out of the window.

'That was in 1960,' she continued, 'and that was it – upped and moved to Japan. We had diplomatic passports, so we weren't allowed to work, but we managed to overcome that. My sister worked as a secretary, and I got a job as a secretary in a travel agency. I met Roger there, in Japan. He was in banking.

'I was over eighteen, so I was on the diplomatic list,' she continued. 'When you're on the diplomatic list, you go to all the national days and official events, and you go to the palace for New Year functions. So, we just got into that sort of decadent lifestyle.'

I asked her if that was how she met Roger.

'Yes, I met him at one of these functions, went out with him once, and, the next time I met up with him, he said, "I think we should get married," and I said, "You better go and see my father."'

She paused and delicately took a sip of her coffee. 'So, my father went to the bank and saw the bank manager and said, "What are the prospects for this chap?" And then my father came home and said, "If you want to marry him, better announce an engagement." So, we did that – and we married six weeks later. I married someone I didn't even know – didn't know anything about him – his habits, his personality, or anything. My father discussed it with us, and he simply said, "I have decided to invite all the Commonwealth ambassadors," and he did. We had an enormous, extravagant, beautiful wedding.'

From the very beginning, I got the impression that June was a bit like a porcelain doll in someone else's enormous luxurious dolls' house. It seemed as though much of her life had been orchestrated around the decisions and wishes of others – typically men – and that her feelings, desires and needs had not played much of a role in dictating the course of her life. Consequently, she seemed to view her emotional needs as though they were a bit of an inconvenience. It was true, however, that she had always been surrounded by luxury and decadence, and had never really wanted for anything in a material sense. She made a point of telling me that she hadn't withdrawn money from a cash machine or a bank in her life and 'wouldn't have the first idea how to use such a machine'.

'Roger has always been in control of the money,' she told

me. 'He always gave me whatever cash he thought I needed. And I always had plenty.'

I sensed that June was under the impression that the fact she had been so materially privileged effectively cancelled out her right to express her wishes in relation to the major decisions of her life, as if her autonomy was a fair price to pay for the privilege she'd been afforded.

But there were times in our conversation when it was abundantly clear that June had sacrificed too much of herself at certain points of her life. She wept as she told me that the hardest thing she'd ever had to do was send their three very young children – Thomas, Evelyn and Jane – away to boarding school on the other side of the world.

'You see, we moved every few years because of Roger's career, so we did three years in Hong Kong, three years in Singapore, three years in Japan, three years in Dubai, three years in Chicago, three years in India, and then back to Hong Kong again. So, we've seen the world.' She sighed. 'But it's not like it didn't come at a price. Yes, the children going to boarding school at five, six and seven years old and just leaving home like that . . . It broke my heart, and it broke their little hearts too.' She wiped her eyes with a decorative lace hanky she pulled from the pocket of her cardigan.

'But Roger couldn't refuse a posting with the bank, you see. You were told, "Your next posting is Brunei." Roger felt we had no choice but to send them away to school,' she remembered. 'The girls sobbed and sobbed one night, and we asked them why they were crying. They thought we'd sent them away to school because we didn't love them, and we were getting rid of them.'

Losing out on the chance to be a full-time mother to her children was something June regretted. She told me she wished she'd been able to be their mother 'in the fullest sense', through the childhood and adolescent years they had spent so far away from each other. Nonetheless, she kept herself busy in the various exotic locations where they lived as Roger's career progressed.

'Sometimes I thought, everything is done for me; what can I do for these people?' she said, as she remembered a procession of cooks, servants and drivers who had served them over the years. 'I wanted to give back. So, in Hong Kong, we set up an orphanage, and unmarried mothers from China would come to Hong Kong, have their babies, go back to China, and then we had to care for these babies until we could get them adopted. That's what I did in Hong Kong.

'In India, we were always going to these beautiful functions, grand parties, with all these rich Indians in saris and dripping in jewellery, and one day I said to a doctor at one of the parties, "Can you tell me who are the poorest of the poor here?" and he said, "It's the people with leprosy." So, I said, "Right, I'd like to work with leprosy."

'So,' she continued, 'I was introduced to doctors that worked in the slums with leprosy and I just worked and worked, for three whole years, with leprosy and the poor. I worked with Mother Teresa, down in the slums. I'd go round all the beds, where all these leprosy patients were, without hands and without feet, and I'd just sit with them, talk to them. I would take fruit or biscuits for them. When the doctors had to do amputations, they would call for me because lepers had no feeling in their limbs and they would just cut them off and drop them in a bucket, and I would just sit, holding their heads, talking to them or distracting them while the doctors went about their work.'

As June described the procession of humanitarian activities that had occupied her time during those years travelling the globe, I couldn't help but marvel at the Forrest Gump-like adventures she'd had.

'In a way,' she told me, 'it was as though I had all this unspent maternal energy and instinct inside me that I wasn't able to direct at my own children at that time. I sometimes wonder if that energy found its way into the world through the work I did with the orphans in Hong Kong and the lepers in India.

'Well,' she continued, 'we finally retired in Hong Kong and said, "Where in the world do we want to live?" And so we got a map of the world and we started putting pins in where we thought we would like to live, whether we wanted to go to New Zealand or stay in the Far East or wherever. We said, "No, we'll come to Britain. Right, let's fly to Edinburgh and find an agent and go house-hunting."

'Oh, I don't know if I should say this,' she said, mildly embarrassed at the lavish lifestyle that would be revealed by what she was about to tell me. 'But, anyway, we bought a castle in the UK. A beautiful Scottish castle. Then, one year, we went on holiday to America, and down there we met some friends who said to us, "Have you seen this new golf resort being built in Florida? You better go and have a look at it." We looked at it and Roger said, "This is the next part of my life. I have always wanted to live in the middle of a golf course." So, we bought a house there next.'

Despite her capacity to care for people in need, June viscerally hated the idea of bothering others with her own wants, needs and desires. And, as our conversation unfolded, the lengths to which she would go to avoid what she thought of as 'inconveniencing others' became increasingly apparent.

'It hurts me to think that anyone had to know what happened to me the other month,' she told me. 'A few people and the police know, but I insisted that nobody tell either Roger or the children.'

A few weeks before our interview, June had gone out for a walk. She'd noticed a man loitering at the gate of the retirement community in which they lived and had approached him to ask if he needed help. He mugged her, violently attacking her and stealing her handbag and purse.

'I like to help people, and I saw that man up there, I thought he was lost, so I went up and said, "Can I help you? Do you want some help?" And that's when he attacked me.' She paused to take a breath. 'I had the keys in my hand, because I have a fob that you have to swipe to get into the club house, here, at the retirement community, and I lost that in the attack, so, when I got away from him, I couldn't get back into the club house. I was downstairs, screaming and banging, and there was a function going on upstairs. It was terrifying. Peter, the manager, came to help me and called the police. It traumatized me a lot.

'In the end,' she continued, 'I felt embarrassed that anyone at all had to get involved with it. It actually really hurt me when the manager quietly gave me some flowers the other day and a message that said, *Hope you're OK*.'

I asked June why such an act of considerate kindness would be hurtful to her.

'I'll tell you why,' she said, becoming more assertive. 'Because I'd rather give, and I don't want other people to give to me. It's that simple.'

In that moment, I could tell she was vehemently defending a world view that she had doggedly clung to for most of her life.

'You know what?' she continued, leaning towards me as though she was about to tell me a secret, 'I'm severely bruised right down this side, after the attack – this shoulder, this arm.' She gestured towards the entire right side of her body. 'And I took all the skin off my knee and bruised my leg terribly, right down here.' She pointed to her thigh and her shin. 'I'm all bruised and battered. And he—' she gestured to the outside world with her left hand, reminding me that Roger was currently out there, somewhere, 'he doesn't know anything about it. That's good, for me, because I don't want to get sympathy. I don't want to burden him with my problems. I never have. I've got this problem and I don't want to pull him down with it too. *No!* I've always been that way.'

There was a pause as we each contemplated and processed what she was saying. I couldn't help but feel a sense of discomfort. There was something unnervingly contradictory about the fact that she could display such enormous compassion towards others, yet seemed to treat herself with what might be described as neglect.

June was compelled to conceal her suffering, even from those closest to her. Professor Andrea Capstick, at the University of Bradford, has argued that many older people, typically born in the first half of the twentieth century, have been indoctrinated into what is commonly known as a 'stiff upper lip' culture.[2] She argues that, through most of their lives, including wartime, peacetime and family life, many people of this generation were routinely required to maintain high levels of cognitive control and low levels of emotional expression. For people like June, this seemed to mean that her feelings, suffering, vulnerability and desires were somehow unimportant, or an inconvenience. June tried to explain to me how she saw it.

'If you don't think about it, if you don't give it words, if you don't alert others to it, then you don't have to feel the pain,' she explained. 'Stiff upper lip – very much part of the background until quite recently. How long is it since men cried in public? Never cry. Big boys don't cry. That is certainly what was said when I was growing up. The emotional side of life has only really been allowed to come forward, I would say, in the last thirty years. I have never seen Roger cry and I don't want him to see me cry either.'

But it seemed to me that the vulnerable and dependent part of June that had been so effectively silenced and hidden was also a consequence of the dominant patriarchal system in which her life had played out. When Professor Capstick wrote about the stiff upper lip, she referred to an idea of masculinity where it was inappropriate for a *man* to lose control or express emotion. June seemed to have been silenced by the expectation that it was her role to dutifully follow the men in her life, regardless of the extent to which it trampled upon her feelings and instincts, or caused her suffering. It felt as though she had been imprisoned in a set of beliefs that were an outgrowth of a gender role she had dutifully fulfilled.

I remembered how the psychotherapist and author, Colette Dowling, had written about what she coined the 'Cinderella complex'. Dowling's book, written in the 1980s, explores the myriad reasons why a woman – although it has since been argued that the concept applies equally to many men – might fear going it alone, have an innate desire to be 'rescued' or 'taken care of', or harbour conscious or unconscious wishes to escape responsibility.[3] The heart of the book considers the consequences of such a complex, demonstrating the ways that being 'wrapped up in cotton wool' can silence, nullify and inhibit a person's growth. In different ways, the Cinderella complex, Dowling argued, can lead to the internalization of ideas that independence is unacceptable, frightening or unfamiliar, or that you are incapable or undeserving of it.

But, despite the fact that she had been 'wrapped up in

cotton wool' for most of her life, June didn't seem to be crying out for a rescuer. In fact, in some ways, she seemed hell-bent on hiding, denying and repressing any vulnerable or dependent sides of her that emerged. The essence of June's loneliness was that she had become completely wedded to the idea that her vulnerable side didn't matter. Her suffering, her needs, her desires and the idea that other people might 'give' to her was not something she could countenance. Her loneliness was connected to a deep-rooted belief that it was desirable to hide her suffering, vulnerability and feelings, to avoid the shame she attached to being dependent or rescued. I wondered whether she'd been so muted, so cosseted, that the idea of any increase in dependency felt like psychological death, as though she would be completely engulfed by it.

'One thing's for certain,' she told me, 'I do *not* want to be a burden on *anyone*, in *any* sense. I don't want someone to have to worry about my problems, or give me tea or sympathy. I don't want, now or in the future, someone to have to dress me, help me, or listen to my worries or woes. And if I can't have it that way? If I can't avoid dependency? Well, honestly, then I would like to think there was euthanasia.'

The look in her eyes gave me no doubt that she was serious. Revealing her vulnerability, depending on others, or, as she put it, having them give to her, was indeed a fate worse than death. For June, vulnerable aspects of her personality were completely relegated to the shadows, split off and hidden away, because she seemed to attach such powerful resistance and shame to them. Unfortunately, our vulnerable selves inevitably show up more and more in later life. I wondered if, in time, old age might eventually be the catalyst that would force June to confront and accept her increasing vulnerability and, albeit reluctantly, let others in.

'What Is a Saddleback?'

Across many different schools of psychology and theories of mind, it is commonly accepted that we consist of 'multiple selves'. In her 2008 book *Multiplicity*, science writer Rita Carter talks about 'major selves' as 'a fully fleshed out character with thoughts, desires, intentions, ambitions, emotions, and beliefs'.[4] She argues that these major selves can sit within us alongside 'minor selves', which might be thought of as a smaller collection of responses that only arise in a particular situation or in relation to a particular issue. She talks about how some of these multiple selves might reflect, for example, 'inner parents' that we have introjected from our early experiences with caregivers. Others might be 'inner children', reflecting states that we were once in during childhood, particularly those attached to powerful experiences like trauma, leaving a terrified or angry inner child floating freely around our soul. We can also internalize roles, such as the fixer, rescuer, teacher, counsellor or victim. And there are undoubtedly darker, more sinister, destructive selves too, the kind we often try to suppress or deny, and that compel us towards what some might consider more noxious behavioural responses and desires.

If you subscribe to that sort of theory of mind, then there's a whole 'farmyard' of selves in each and every one of us. Sometimes they can take the helm and steer the ship for a while, sometimes they lay dormant, sometimes they may be in conflict with each other, and sometimes they may demand attention to the extent that you cannot ignore them. If you get to know them – get to know yourself – then it's highly likely that some of these selves are deeply lonely, floating around in there with little acknowledgement, constantly repressed or defended against, yet imbued with unique and powerful experiences of loneliness. That's what I discovered in my mum. There's a lonely little girl inside her with a story to tell, and she's been hiding, alone, since 1958, at the bottom of a garden somewhere in rural Hertfordshire.

There are people who fall through the cracks in the education system. For whatever reason, their gifts, talents and what they have to offer the world go unnoticed, remain unseen or are suffocated out of them. If you haven't been in their shoes, it can be difficult to appreciate what this feels like.

I was telling Mum about a research project I was working on – a series of retrospective interviews about older people's experiences of taking the eleven-plus exam in the 1950s. We were in the kitchen of the basement flat I rented when we first moved to Bath. I thought it would be romantic, in a sort of Jane Austen sense, to live in one of the honey-coloured crescents that are dotted around the city of Bath, so we rented the basement in a beautiful Georgian house that was owned and occupied by the former UK ambassador for Chile, who would sometimes invite me upstairs for a glass of sherry in the drawing room with him and his wife. He was almost deaf, but that didn't really matter, as he didn't seem to want any audible input from me – so long as I nodded, smiled and seemed to enjoy the sherry.

In the kitchen that day, it was obvious that there was something about the research project that resonated with Mum. In truth, when I'm talking about my research with friends or family, it's often clear to me that they're only half engaged. I'll get the sense that they aren't really listening, at least not with any attention to detail or genuine enthusiasm. But something about that particular project caught Mum's attention.

After the Second World War, the 1944 Education Act sought to reform secondary education in England and Wales. Based on the outcome of what amounted to a rigid end-of-primary-school 'intelligence' test, children were channelled towards either a grammar-school education or a 'technical' or 'secondary modern' school. Interestingly, the idea was heavily based upon psychologists' belief at the time that each child possessed an innate, unalterable intelligence that dictated their suitability for either an academic, technical or functional secondary education. The eleven-plus exam determined which pathway they were best suited to.

In our study, we were interested in the idea that the eleven-plus was an educational experience that shaped key aspects of people's character and identity. As the humanities scholar Professor Jacky Brine suggested, it was the pivotal point of selection – a key moment in constructing the dispositions of children as either bright and successful, or 'thick' and a failure.[5] And Mum clearly had a story to tell about it.

Before I knew it, she had persuaded me to dig out my Dictaphone and had poured us each a glass of lemonade that we took into the garden. And, on that beautiful sunny afternoon in Bath, we sat side by side on a decorative wrought-iron bench in the idyllic gated communal gardens attached to our crescent, and my mum opened up and told me her story. We were surrounded by large rose bushes, a variety of trees and exotic-looking plants. When I listen to the tape recording of our conversation, I can even hear the birds and a large bumblebee or two in the background.

She spoke in an animated and passionate way from the beginning, and I felt as though the story she was telling me was perhaps being told for the first time. She had certainly never told us about this when we were growing up and I felt a little taken aback that there was something, or perhaps someone, so powerful inside her that I didn't know much about.

'Something definitely changed at about seven or eight years old,' she reflected. 'My brother was involved in this eleven-plus thing, and I heard all the talking about it. That's when it became something in my head too. I realized that this thing he was going through was going to happen to me too!' She paused and took another sip of her lemonade. 'I saw that my brother hated it. For some reason, *I* was getting nervous watching *him* go through it. But he passed. I saw how great that was to Dad, and I'd got all that to go through myself.'

Mum was very clear that Grandpa had made quite a big deal of the eleven-plus.

'The eleven-plus meant, or at least *Dad* had made it mean, absolutely everything. He always said, "Oh, you'll walk through that." He thought it was so important in life and he didn't realize how unhappy and worried it made me.'

She continued, 'I had it ingrained in my head that entry into grammar school was the best thing – no, the only thing – to do, if you wanted to do well. It seemed as though that was all they ever talked about. Apparently, it meant that you were supposedly clever, intelligent, and passing the eleven-plus *made* you intelligent and successful . . . and, if you failed, you were no good.

'You know, I always thought I was *good* at maths and writing and that!' she said, with a sense of disbelief. 'I would never go home from school thinking, God, I can't do that. But then, almost overnight, I felt like a complete and total failure. I felt like I was no good at anything. And that all started with my eleven-plus.

'Do you know, I can't even remember *taking* the eleven-plus,' she reflected. 'But I can remember the day the letter came, and I hadn't passed. I can remember the letter arriving. I can remember running down to the bottom of the garden, crying my eyes out and hiding.'

At this point, I sensed anger and pain emerging in her voice as she grappled with the injustice of it all.

'Why? Because I felt like shit! I didn't want to see anyone. I felt a total failure. I remember the thing coming in the post and opening it, or Dad opening it, saying something like,' she put on a stern, deep voice as she tried to impersonate Grandpa, '"You've not been successful . . . errr . . . I'll look into this." I just ran away. I was thinking how I'd let everybody down, how I didn't meet requirements, as a daughter or as a person. I just wanted to run away because I felt so upset.'

I realized that day just what a momentous experience the eleven-plus had been for Mum, and I felt a deep sense of sadness for her as she told me about it. Certain things started to make a little more sense. I realized, for example, how significant her story was in explaining why it had always seemed so desperately important to her that we, her children, felt as though we were 'successful' in the realm of education.

'It was such a big kick in the teeth because I thought it was very important,' she continued. 'Deep down, I suppose I thought Dad didn't love me because of it. I'm sure he did, but that's what I thought. I felt less of a person too. This was all they ever talked about. It was always just thrown at me . . . and it was a *shock* . . . it was a *shock* to him, the school and me that I didn't make it. I was always scared that I would never measure up to expectations, and now I knew that I didn't, I knew that I wasn't that "clever, capable child".'

She paused at this point as we both processed the significance of what she was saying. I remember staring at some large pink-and-white roses, searching for the right response.

'After I failed, they let me go to an interview for the eleven-plus. Dad had "specially arranged" it, because he was a teacher and he knew people in the right places. It was like a second chance to pass the eleven-plus,' she reflected. 'He should never have done that. In the end, it meant I failed twice, and it was a big enough thing for me just once. But I was pleased because I thought, Oooh, great – I'm going to be doing something right!'

I asked her what the 'interview' involved.

'Well, I had to go in, spend fifteen minutes to half an hour with the headmaster and someone else, and they asked me questions. I can remember one of the questions that I got wrong. They asked me what a "saddleback" was. It was a pig, but I didn't know it was a pig, so I got that wrong. But I've known ever since,' she replied.

I smiled, somewhat uncomfortably, at the absurdity of the fact that such pivotal moments in life can hinge upon knowing what a saddleback is. I googled 'saddleback' that afternoon – I'm ashamed to say that, even as an adult, I wasn't completely sure what it was either – and learned that they are large, lop-eared, deep-bodied pigs, with predominantly black bodies and a white band around the saddle and front legs.

Mum continued, 'Then I found out that result . . . a failure still. I felt my self-esteem had reached zero. And did I get over it? I don't think I did. I never got over it. I'm sorry, but I'm going to cry in a minute. I'm sorry . . . just give me a minute.'

And then she wept about something that, up to that point, I'd had no idea had been so deeply wounding for her. I was witnessing, first hand, just how painful experiences of educational failure can be. Mum's wounded sense of self felt just as raw in that moment as I imagined it had when she ran to the bottom of the garden crying as an eleven-year-old child.

'I think it affected me for the rest of my life, the fact that I was second best. I was "injured" by it,' she said. 'I think I never again trusted – no, that's not the right word – I never again allowed myself to believe – and, before that, I *did* believe – that I was going to be successful.'

Sighing dejectedly, she wiped her eyes with a tissue that she pulled out of her bag. I felt as though the crushed, injured, suppressed little girl inside her was talking.

'I wasn't going to try to go to university and I wasn't going to try to do this or that ever again, because I was frightened of that awful feeling. And the terrible truth is that's gone through my life. Jobs, for example – I can do jobs well, but I've never wanted to strive for more, because I felt I wasn't capable of it.'

The philosophy professor, Sandra Bartky, argues that, when we think about people as 'oppressed', we most often have something political or economic in mind. But she notes that people *can* be oppressed psychologically, and a key feature of oppression is its psychological internalization. 'The psychologically oppressed,' she writes, 'become their own oppressors', because they internalize what she calls 'intimations of inferiority'.[6]

In a sense, that's what Mum's story was about. Her recollections came from a part of her, a lonely inner child, who had long ago internalized an idea that she wasn't good enough. Somewhere during that painful eleven-plus episode, a part of her had come to believe insinuations that she was incapable, incompetent, 'thick' or 'stupid'. These insinuations had crystallized, casting a shadow over the course of her life. Parts of Mum, parts of her that might have had the opportunity to shine, to thrive, to flourish, to develop and to grow, had been shut away, unharnessed and lost to the world. As a little child, Mum had run to the bottom of the garden and hidden. A small part of her, a lonely self, has been hiding down at the bottom of the garden ever since.

'I'm a bit of a film buff,' he told me. 'That's an understate-
ment, actually. I find that there's always a film I can pull out
of the bag that captures the essence of what I'm feeling or
offers me a metaphor of some kind.'

Will was just twenty-three years old – a student – and he
had volunteered to be interviewed about his experience of
heartbreak. As a relationship scholar, I've always been fascinated by the idea of 'relational death'. The psychoanalyst John
Bowlby called his seminal work *Attachment and Loss*, an
acknowledgement of the central role of both the making *and*
breaking of human connections. As he sat opposite me on a
standard-issue office chair, Will looked categorically dejected.
He was wearing a pin-striped blazer with a small Bob Dylan
badge on the lapel, a white T-shirt underneath, blue jeans
and a pair of adidas Sambas in blue suede. His clean-shaven,
handsome and youthful face could not disguise the fact that
he was suffering. He gave off the aura of someone who was
carrying a heavy emotional burden.

'I feel like a shell of my former self,' he informed me.
'From the moment she told me, literally, I just shattered into
a million tiny pieces and I'm just a husk of a person right
now.'

He said it with a sense of conviction that left me in little
doubt that he meant it. Heartbreak is an extremely serious
matter. Depth psychologist, Ginette Paris, has pointed out
that 'there is something final and tragic about losing your

partner to death', but it is not typically a 'personal affront'.[7] In contrast, mourning the loss of somebody who *chooses* to leave you is a unique kind of insult to the ego. There is an intentional abandonment that can sting more acutely than losses brought about by death.

Will's first love, Melissa, had left him just three months ago. They had been together since he was seventeen and had shared a six-year relationship that started in sixth-form college when he sat next to her in an A-level geography class.

'I was watching something on Netflix, and enjoying it, and then her text popped up on my phone. It was full of those nondescript, bullshit phrases that reflect the fact that she's about to stab you in the side with a sharp knife. You know, things like "we'll always be friends", "I'll always love you", and "who knows what the future will hold". They're just bullshit; she's simultaneously breaking my heart and telling me it'll all be OK. You know?'

He looked at me for reassurance. I nodded. I thought that I knew what he meant.

'Anyway,' he continued, 'I called her back immediately and tried to work out what was going on. I know things had been difficult, that wasn't a surprise to me, and we'd talked about the possibility of ending, but I hadn't got there yet, not in my own head.' He reflected for a moment. 'So, she picked up the phone when I called, and I asked her if we could at least sit down together and talk, sort this out. She just sounded . . . different . . . and I sensed something was very wrong. I just sort of *knew*. I asked her to please tell me this wasn't about someone else, because that would break my heart into even tinier pieces than the end of the relationship alone, possibly grinding it into a fine dust. She couldn't tell me it wasn't about someone else.'

I could feel that Will's trauma was still very raw.

'She told me she'd joined a dating site, was already "talking to other people". I mean, *what the fuck?* We hadn't even drawn a line under things, and she's already window shopping.' He shook his head in disbelief. 'Well, from that moment, I sort of forgot how on earth I'd found any joy in the Netflix series I was watching. All conceptualization of joy, happiness, excitement – it all just faded away in an instant. The whole world turned grey, and I haven't worked out how to turn the colour back on.

'The next fucking day she went on a date, posting all over Facebook how excited she was. And, that same weekend, while I'm still talking to her, and she's telling me she's willing to talk, loves me, looks me in the eye, sees how broken I am, allows me to tie myself in knots trying to repair and protect what we have . . . And she hummed and hawed about us? Well, while all that is going on, she lied to me, tells me she's going away with friends "to think", but ran off with this fucking new dude from the internet for the weekend,' he said incredulously. 'I'm telling you, she became someone else in the space of a week. Cold. Callous. Unresponsive. And I feel like I metamorphosed from someone she *loved* into a traumatized nuisance that she would rather see the back of, because it simply made her feel guilty and bad about herself to even look at me.

'You've seen the film *Ghost*, right?' He looked at me for confirmation.

'Patrick Swayze and Demi Moore, 1990? I've seen it a few times.'

Satisfied with my response, he nodded and continued. 'Well, then you'll know the plotline of that film, which really sums up how I feel right now. It's the whole part where Patrick Swayze is murdered and becomes a ghost. And the woman he loves, Demi Moore, simply can't see him any longer – he's invisible to her *because* he's a ghost and, in a literal sense, I suppose, he is dead to her – and there's this whole sad plot line where he is no longer visible to the woman he loves.' He paused. 'That's exactly how it feels to me, as though I suddenly turned into a ghost and Melissa just . . . stopped seeing me. Does that sound crazy?'

I shook my head. It didn't sound crazy to me.

'Ghost' – I looked it up that evening in the *O.E.D.* It's defined as 'the apparition of a dead person, which is believed to appear or become manifest to the living, typically as a nebulous image attempting to right a wrong done in life'.

I had been there too, and the *Ghost* analogy made perfect sense to me. As Will paused in his story, I remembered in a blinding flash the times in my life when women I had deeply loved, and had been utterly convinced had deeply loved me too, had suddenly stopped seeing me as someone they loved and had transitioned into a person I no longer recognized almost overnight. There had been times when it felt as though a partner had shed their skin like a snake, unzipping and peeling away an entire layer of themselves, a layer that somehow contained all of their feelings for me, and emerging as a new version, a 'mark 2.0', who simply did not love me any more. I became invisible to them, like a ghost they could not see, a nebulous apparition trying desperately to remind them that I was someone they used to love. There was something agonizingly lonely about the experience. I recognized it in Will's account. It's the essence of what terrifies us so much about dementia, or the plot lines of zombie movies, the idea that someone we love deeply can be *physically* present, yet somehow devoid of the spirit inside them that once enabled them to *see* us as unique, special and loveable.

'I honestly felt like nobody in the entire world could help me,' he continued. 'They couldn't. I called Mum, Dad, my sister, my friends. I wept, they tried to console me, but I felt like nobody had any idea how it felt to lose all meaning in life in an instant. They meant well, they said things like "you won't always feel this way", "you just have to move on" and "it's for the best". But it didn't help. I felt like a helpless animal caught in one of those cruel traps that are like barrels of water, when they fall into the barrel and scrabble around at the sides, with absolutely no foothold, until they eventually give up and die by drowning.

'I was so panicked, so traumatized, those first few nights. I left my flat and just walked around the city all night.' He stared into space, as if remembering the experience. 'And the city that has always felt like "home" to me, suddenly didn't feel like home any more. I felt lost. I called Grandad and he tried to comfort me. But he couldn't. I walked around with a bottle of whisky in a brown paper bag, trying to numb the terror.

'In the end, I wound up at the Samaritans office at one o'clock in the morning. A man who looked like he was in his sixties, Joel, with a kind face and a grey beard, opened the door, invited me in, and sat and listened to me, after making me a cup of tea,' Will explained. 'He could see I was beside myself, and he told me that, even though he was supposed to simply listen, he'd break the rules on this occasion and tell me about the times he'd been abandoned by women he loved. It had happened to him four times over the course of his life. I felt comforted by the fact that he was still alive, because I didn't even think I'd make it through the night. It was excruciating.'

*

According to the psychologist and therapist Ginette Paris, 'we resort to metaphor each time we need to explain something unfamiliar or mysterious by comparing it to something familiar or simple'.[8] The shades of loneliness that so often accompany experiences of heartbreak, abandonment and betrayal, like Will described, lend themselves well to such metaphor. A friend once described his experience of a heartbreak similar to Will's: 'it was like I was blotted out of a masterpiece and replaced as easily as I was painted in'. I have heard people describe the grief associated with heartbreak as 'a round Rubik's cube that I couldn't understand how to begin', 'a wolf that stands on our throat and stares into our eyes as it devours our heart', 'a barren desert in which we are lost and weary' and 'an avalanche that buries us alive'.

Understanding the inner experiences people are trying to convey through the use of such metaphor is complex. They describe a process of psychological death that is traumatic, lonely and difficult to comprehend for outsiders. According to the Jungian analyst Aldo Carotenuto, when someone breaks our heart, there is an immediate collapse of a kind of psychological order. In the collapse, we lose who we were *for* our lover, who we were *with* them and who we were *to* them. In getting so close to someone else's psychological world, we have inevitably structured ourselves differently and been modified by the very need to unite with another human being. In heartbreak, Carotenuto explains, 'this set-up is overturned, and fundamental aspects of our existence are called into question. What can one do in these desperate moments? Each affair has its own special identity and there are no points of reference in the external world. No words can reach us, no change of scene console.'[9] Such a collapse necessitates psychological death, loss of identity and the crumbling of an idea of ourselves. And what could be lonelier than that?

For Will, there was perhaps an added layer of horror in the fact that this was his first experience of the barren landscape in which he now found himself.

'If I hear one more well-meaning person tell me to "just move on",' he told me, 'then I'm going to scream. Because, answer me this, what the hell does "move on" even mean? I feel like my entire identity, the direction my life was headed, who I thought I was – it's all been erased with a great big whiteboard rubber. So, where do I move on? Towards what? And how? People don't seem to understand that.'

Will had raised his voice slightly, in both tone and pitch, in a way that helped me to appreciate his sense of desperation. His frustration reflected the fact that heartbreak can feel a bit like the map for your life has been snatched away, torn into little pieces and set alight in front of you. And there you are, rudderless, without the map, and with no coordinates for where to head next.

'I just need to know that this is not how I'm going to feel for the rest of my life,' he said, panicked, 'because right now it feels like it might be, and I don't seem to be able to make it stop – nobody does.'

Ginette Paris has argued that being lost in the desert, like Will and the millions of others in the midst of the agonizing loneliness of heartbreak, is often a 'necessary push from nature'. That is, the pain, loneliness and suffering seem to propel most of us towards the possibility for an 'evolutionary jump'. What that means is that the mere exposure to such acute existential crisis and radical change *requires* us to adapt, or, in a very real sense, we wither and die. As Paris puts it, 'recovery is not, as so many are tempted to believe, a simple decision to "move on", an emotional shutting down, or a closing of the heart'. Rather, it only happens 'if the heart can continue its painful expansion and stays open until one learns something crucial about love and relationships'. The desert *can* be crossed, there *is* another side, and the journey, although lonely, horrifying and fraught with suffering, has much to teach us.

I've been in Will's shoes and it's hard to articulate how it feels to be in that place. Once, when I was in the throes of the crushing grief associated with a particularly painful heartbreak, a good friend and psychotherapist asked me if I *really* knew how a caterpillar transitions into a butterfly. As we sat outside her cottage, with a mug of tea, looking up at the starry August sky, I muttered something about the caterpillar becoming a chrysalis and the process sort of kicking off from there. I was vague because I knew about the transition itself but not the specifics behind how it came about.

'No, but do you know what *actually* happens in there?' she challenged me.

I felt like a schoolchild under pressure and was forced to admit that, no, I didn't *really* know what happened.

Ostensibly, she explained, the caterpillar eats and eats, and creates the chrysalis in which it eventually becomes cocooned. 'It's what happens in there that's miraculous!' she enthused. 'The caterpillar produces enzymes to essentially break itself down into a sort of "soup". It literally "breaks down", so that all of its cells still exist, but in a big, sloppy, caterpillar soup.'

She told me that some of the cells, called 'imaginal discs', *know* where to float to, and seem to find their way to the right places, where they will eventually scaffold the process of forming wings and other core structures. Somehow, out of the soup, the butterfly is born and has the task of eating its way out of the cocoon.

'And, of course,' she continued, 'you can't rush the process. If you were to mistakenly try to help the butterfly, by breaking the cocoon open while it's eating its way out, for example, you'd be messing with the natural developmental rhythm, and it would not survive or develop as it should. It has to be as it has to be.' She paused. 'Well, my friend, right now, in the midst of your heartbreak, *you* are that "soup". Your old life, as a caterpillar, as the person you once knew yourself to be, has been deconstructed, broken down, lost, and you *are* that soup.'

It made sense to me. I felt like a soup. I lacked structure, like a pool of liquid that simply couldn't hold its form.

I told Will the story. He reflected on it.

'Well, I can't tell you how much I hate being a soup,' he told me. 'I want to run back to being a caterpillar, where I know what my life looks like. I don't know what form I will take in the future or what kind of butterfly I'm going to be.'

In time, I had every confidence he'd learn what sort of butterfly he'd be. But I understood his scepticism. I wasn't so certain either, when I was in his shoes. Scepticism seems to be a fundamental part of being the soup.

'Achingly Graceful'

It was not so long into our relationship – maybe three months or so – and Natalie's foot suddenly started to twitch under the duvet. It was involuntary and impossible not to notice. It was as though her foot had a mind of its own and was violently shivering. I instinctively knew that it was her body's way of flagging something urgent, something significant, something over which she clearly had little power or control. In time, I'd learn that her twitching foot was a manifestation of deeply hidden anxieties and fears that surfaced from time to time, often without warning. As I held her that first time, she started to shake, as though the twitching in her foot had spread up her leg and into her entire body. Then she told me, bluntly and coolly, rather like a robot, that when she was a child she was horrifically abused, and someone – he – made her do unspeakable things that no child should ever have to endure. It felt as though the robotic delivery of the information was the only way she could tell me without exploding. That afternoon, she cried in my arms until the feelings of terror, fear and anxiety subsided and her body seemed calmer. I cried too, but I didn't let her see me crying because I felt as though it was *her* moment.

As I learned about her childhood, I couldn't help but be affected by what she'd endured. It was difficult to comprehend that, for the duration of her childhood and young adult life, she had been alone with the memories and profound impact of those traumatic experiences. For much of her childhood, she told me, nobody knew – not her family, her friends, or even a therapist. She was in every sense wholly alone with fragmented memories she often didn't know had even been a part of her life until they would surface like wild beasts emerging from the depths of the forest. She had endured experiences that were tormenting, terrifying and deeply disturbing. The psychiatrist and author, Bessel van der Kolk, writes in *The Body Keeps the Score* that 'silence about trauma leads to death – death of the soul. Silence reinforces the godforsaken isolation of trauma.'[10] By allowing me to know and love her, Natalie permitted me to glimpse shades of the loneliness that stems from childhood experiences of complex trauma. I'll always be in awe of her strength, resilience and capacity to transform her life into something that I hope will end more happily than it began.

At first, I hadn't registered the little signs that, buried deep inside her, she carried the fragments of a heartbreaking story of childhood trauma and abuse. One day, while we were still getting to know each other, I had noticed her walking down the street, so I'd pulled over to say 'Hi' and have a chat. As the sun shone down on her tanned, slender arms, I noticed for the first time a mishmash of horizontal white scars adorning the skin of her forearms and wrists. They glistened in the sun. Each scar was no more than a couple of centimetres in length and there were occasional scars that ran diagonally across the horizontal ones, ruining any semblance of symmetry and order. There are many reasons for scarification of the body. In regions of central Ghana, for example, fetish priests mark people's arms or wrists to protect them from evil. In other parts of the world, it can occur for reasons deemed medicinal, decorative, or for tribal and familial identification. I instinctively knew that Natalie's scars had not been carved for any of these reasons. I noticed them, but I didn't mention them. I don't know if she noticed that I noticed.

Later, she told me that she wished more people would acknowledge or ask her about her scars, because she does notice that people notice them. Her boss noticed them at work, but didn't say anything; she registered the scars, then, in a split second, made the decision that it was none of her business, or was inappropriate to talk about. Natalie told me that she understands people don't want to draw attention to something they worry she might find distressing or uncomfortable. But, at the same time, it also felt to her like yet another instance where the desperate, terrified, angry, confused teenager – who took to cutting herself over and over again, before finally attempting to take her life and spending a chunk of her adolescence in the care of various institutions – is ignored or relegated to the margins of consciousness.

I don't have a clear idea of everything he did to Natalie as a child – neither does she – at least not with perfect clarity or coherence. Trauma theorists like van der Kolk have argued that dissociation – a disruption in consciousness, identity, perception and memory during and following traumatic episodes – means that memory fragmentation and disturbances are quite common.[11] High levels of powerful emotion and dissociation that often occur during traumatic experiences have been found to disrupt memory in a variety of ways. This can range from complete amnesia to disorganized or disintegrated recall, or uncontrollable memory intrusions. Natalie once told me that it feels a bit like her brain, long ago, frantically sought to tear large parts of that traumatic childhood narrative into tiny little pieces, hurriedly scattering and burying them in the depths of her body and mind.

Pretending they didn't exist was the only way to survive. She said she knows terrible things happened and the story is in there somewhere, but she can't access the pieces coherently. Consequently, she frequently stumbles upon fragments of her childhood that can terrify and disturb her without warning and are deeply distressing when they invade the present moment.

The upshot of this is that life can feel like a bit of a minefield because she can never quite predict what will trigger the emergence of something terrifying, dark and sinister. It could be the sight of a spider on the wall or ceiling that makes her scream with terror, provoking memories of how he forced her, as a petrified child, to put her hands into cavities in the wall, which were laden with white, silky egg sacs, to disturb the spiders, so he could feed them to his pet tarantula. One night, as we drove along a dark country lane, returning to our hotel after sharing a romantic meal, she became fixated on the idea that a fictional character from a series of horror movies was hiding in the back of the car. As she calmed down, she remembered how he forced her, as a small powerless child, to watch the movie, or be sent upstairs for a punishment that no child should ever endure. The movie, like spiders, has forever been imbued with the horror, cruelty and depravity that characterized those early traumatic experiences.

From my perspective, when they surfaced, these fragments of memory and emotion were palpable. I mean to say that I could feel them too, as though they were in the room with us on a hidden wavelength that temporarily hijacked our sensory and emotional apparatus. Therapists use the term 'vicarious' or 'secondary' trauma to describe the impact of empathically engaging with graphic and traumatizing material that is part of another person's narrative. Secondary exposure to deep levels of human cruelty through the re-enactment of trauma can be extremely powerful.

Once, as we drove through the city on a weekday after-noon, Natalie suddenly asked me to pull over because she had experienced a deeply distressing physical memory. She told me that her memories are not always visual and some-times the first re-enactment of a traumatic memory might be a powerful physical sensation, which may or may not be fol-lowed by visual, auditory or verbal clues that help her to fill in the gaps. In the car that day, she experienced a physical sensation associated with the abuse. She sat, petrified and disorientated, as she desperately tried to make sense of what her body was experiencing and to work out how to cope with it. I held her in my arms as the procession of afternoon traffic drove past our Nissan Micra. I felt shocked, numb, angry, nauseous, sad, slightly shaky and completely floored by that little fragment of memory. I could not begin to imagine how she must have felt.

Being alone takes on a different complexion when you are never quite certain what terrors might emerge from within. Natalie and I talked about it a lot over the years and tried to make sense of it together. She once told me that it feels as though she's floating in a boat on a vast body of water. In her mind, if she looks down at the water, she can see threatening, sinister, dark shapes moving around beneath the surface. She is reminded of what's lurking down there and that it could emerge at any moment.

Once, I asked her if she could articulate the loneliness that comes from the traumatic experiences she endured. Her answer, as is so often the case, was profound. She told me the loneliness that arises from the trauma she experienced comes from the unpredictable nature of the fragments of memory that lurk beneath the surface. They make it feel riskier to be alone because she can never be sure if or when they might arise. The closeness and comfort of other people helps to combat any emotional trauma that might arise; it feels safer to be around others you know and trust.

She has a particular childhood memory of an autumnal evening during the height of the abuse. She was safely at home, in the company of friends and family who loved her. She glanced out of the window and something about the fading light reminded her that it was that time of the day – when her parents usually drove her there, to the child-minder's. She suddenly experienced a spine-tingling sensation, an agonizing feeling of loneliness related to being in a room filled with people who loved her, yet knowing that these people would soon deliver her to other people who would subject her to the cruellest levels of sexual and emotional abuse. She wanted to tell them. She wanted to scream at them to save her. She longed to stay with them, to remain safe – but she couldn't. He told her he would kill her family if she shared their secret. So, she suffered alone, in silence, for their sakes.

In her childhood, a unique kind of loneliness developed. It was a feeling others will know too: that you are deeply unsafe, that there *are* people who love you, and *could* plausibly save you, but that you can't reach out to them.

Natalie told me that somebody once described her as 'achingly graceful'. We laughed about it, but a lot of people have said that about her, about how she moves like a ballerina. And I have heard other people remark on an aura of 'grace' and 'dignity' that surrounds her. In *Man's Search for Meaning*, Viktor Frankl chronicles what he learned from his experiences as a prisoner in Nazi concentration camps during the Second World War. He carefully describes the demoralization and indignity that comes from near constant exposure to being dehumanized by extreme cruelty. In one passage, he explains how he lined up with a large group of starving, emaciated prisoners to receive a small daily ration of bread. Their line was disorderly and asymmetrical because many prisoners were too weak to stand or were unable to maintain their balance. Suddenly, he felt a sharp blow to the side of his head and realized that he had been struck violently with a stick by a guard who had taken offence to the fact that the man behind him wasn't standing straight. He writes, 'At such a moment it is not the physical pain which hurts the most . . . it is the mental agony caused by the injustice, the unreasonableness of it all.'[12] He describes how, sometimes, in the face of such cruelty and mental torment, people still held onto a sense of grace and dignity that could not be taken away from them. 'In a position of utter desolation,' he continues, 'sometimes our most profound achievements may consist in enduring our suffering in the right way – an honourable way.'

Perhaps there is also a dignity to be found in the way we ride out to meet our loneliness when it comes calling.

PART THREE

ESCAPE

The Cricket Bat

I met Adil some years ago, during a research project that involved working with unaccompanied asylum-seeking children. He was fourteen years old. It was hard to believe that, two months earlier, he'd been discovered underneath a tarpaulin, hiding in the back of a lorry, in a service station on the M4 motorway. He had made a pretty treacherous escape from Afghanistan and somehow wound up in Bristol. He wasn't alone when we first met him. There were six unaccompanied asylum-seeking children in the foster agency in Bristol that week. In that year, in March alone, there had been around 4,216 such children arriving in the UK in need of local-authority care. My colleagues and I were holding a focus group for potential foster carers, and one of them was quick to state her case.

'I am not racist by no means, but I just got something up in my head that all these children, or so-called children, trying to come over here, well, I refuse to foster any of them, because I have just got it up here in my head that they will be up in their bedrooms making bombs,' Sally told us, animatedly.

She was a plump, tired-looking woman, with a kindly face. I noticed that she kept her red coat on for the duration of the session.

'Look, don't ask me why, but I am being honest. I just got it up here,' she said, firmly tapping her index finger against her temple. 'From our point of view, watching the news, you seen all the men coming across, don't you, on lorries, and you do worry about terrorism.'

A couple of the other foster carers – a middle-aged man, also still wearing his coat, and a slightly younger woman with blonde hair tied back in a ponytail with a luminous pink scrunchy – nodded and made sounds of agreement.

The first purpose of our project was to explore the barriers that would-be UK foster carers had around fostering unaccompanied asylum-seeking children, because the agency had informed us that it was proving increasingly difficult to place children like Adil. The staff at the agency were run off their feet and seemed genuinely pleased that we might be able to help them tackle the issue. Simply listening to the concerns, thoughts and feelings of people like Sally and the other local foster carers enabled us to see that the agency's suspicions were correct – a wall of prejudice was significantly hindering their capacity to find willing, compassionate foster carers for Adil and other children like him.

We met the boys themselves on a dark, wet winter evening, in the meeting room at the foster agency. Our second aim was simply to get to know them and, over time, build some sort of relationship with them. Our project leader and the team at the foster agency thought that it might be a good idea to offer weekly workshops for the boys that would enable them to engage with a wide range of creative and physical activities. There is also quite a lot of evidence in the academic literature that creative therapies can be very helpful in healing some of the wounds related to the trauma that refugee children frequently experience. Over time, by documenting their experiences with them – taking photographs, building collages and simply getting to know them through the various creative and physical media – the agency hoped that potential foster carers might be better able to appreciate the children as more than the set of projected prejudices, and that people would perhaps be more willing to offer unaccompanied asylum-seeking children a foster home. At least, that was the plan.

When we met the boys for the first time, it felt a bit like a press conference. We were sitting at a big, shiny table in the agency's meeting room, and there were different interpreters to cater for the fact that the boys spoke a range of languages, from Albanian to Pashto. When they entered the room, one after the other, I was surprised to see that they were evidently already attending UK schools. Adil was wearing the uniform for a secondary school in Weston-super-Mare: polished black shoes, blazer, crisp white shirt and tie, and smart black trousers. The others had different uniforms, and none of them attended the same school. Adil was small for a fourteen-year-old. He had a youthful face and a crop of scruffy black hair. His file made for sobering reading. As far as the agency could tell, his family had been murdered by men with machetes who'd come to his village, and this may well have been something Adil had witnessed – he was currently unwilling to talk about it. He was terrified that the people who had killed his family would eventually kill him too. He had fled his country for his life. The agency believed he had likely had an extremely traumatic migration experience that involved abuse and exploitation. He spoke Pashto and very little English. The other children's files were similar, in the sense that they reflected a litany of trauma, horror and turbulence.

In my mind, I couldn't quite reconcile the facts. Adil had, by all accounts, spent the day in a classroom somewhere in Weston-super-Mare, learning about ratio, algebra and the reign of Elizabeth I in a language he could hardly speak, when, just a couple of months ago, he had been hiding in the back of a lorry, in a foreign country, fearing for his life following the slaughter of his family. As I looked at the children across the table, I had an uncomfortable feeling, because I wasn't sure how 'willing' they really were to be trussed up in school uniforms and thrust into a completely different world, so soon after such traumatic experiences, without any sort of transition period or opportunity to catch a breath. I wondered whether or not it was in their best interests, and they looked like fish out of water. But the staff at the agency told us the boys really wanted to attend school and were extremely happy to be learning again.

We talked to the boys through their interpreters and translators, explained that we'd like to work with them, and offered them the opportunity to ask questions and decide whether or not they'd like to be involved. They all said that they did want to be part of the project, and together we worked out a schedule of workshops and activities that we could engage in over the course of the next few weeks. We planned art workshops, photography sessions, nature-based activities, and a variety of sports and leisure opportunities, like football and rock climbing.

I liked Adil and I sensed that he liked me too. It just seemed as though we got on well. That evening, when the interpreters and translators had gone home, our team, the youth workers and the boys were left to get to know each other over tea and refreshments. Our conversation amounted to Adil showing me where he was from on a map, asking me to show him where I was from, and each of us naming different famous sportspeople we knew, like Michael Jordan, David Beckham or Usain Bolt, until we were both seemingly delighted whenever we identified something we had in common, however mundane.

As I drove home from the agency that night, I couldn't help but feel overwhelmed at how challenging life must have been for Adil. He had lost, in the most traumatic way, the relationships that he had relied upon, up to this point, for love, support and a sense of belonging. He had, to a large extent, lost his identity. His capacity to communicate with the world around him was now restricted and he also carried the burden of terrifying traumatic experiences that he hadn't yet been able to share and was completely alone with.

In a 2008 paper, Dr Nigar Khawaja and colleagues from the School of Psychology and Counselling at Queensland University of Technology, in Australia, have summarized the uniquely intense experiences of loneliness that many refugees encounter. They outline a whole raft of issues, including feeling like an alien in a new culture, adaptation demands such as language barriers, the challenge of becoming familiar with new cultural values and ideals, learning how to access resources, difficulties forming new social relationships, and the complete or partial loss of one's culture, family and social network.[1] It amounts to an extraordinary sense of isolation.

All of the boys turned up for the first workshop the following week. An artist, Beatrice, was unloading all sorts of supplies from her car when we arrived. When she was ready, we gathered around her in a room at the foster agency. She had taped an enormous piece of paper to the wall and started to use a collection of spray-paints to create something. She worked purposefully, reminding me of the artists I used to watch on TV in childhood, who would skilfully create amazing pictures out of something like rice or sand. We all watched her as though we were gathered around a street performer. After a while, it became apparent that she was painting a huge blue whale with the spray-paints, and everyone in the room was really impressed. The boys made remarks in Pashto or Albanian that sounded as though they were compliments, and we occasionally all looked at each other and made facial expressions that further confirmed how much we were all appreciating her work.

When she had finished, we gave her a round of applause. And that's when the session nosedived. Beatrice had had the idea that the boys would be so moved and motivated by her painting that it would inspire them to have a go themselves, and that their creations would provide rich and important material through which we could begin to connect to them and understand them. It didn't work out that way. Sure, they clearly thought the whale was a great piece of art. So did I. But they weren't suddenly going to pick up the spray cans and start 'opening up' through the medium of graffiti. Instead, they steadfastly refused to have a go, no matter how profusely the slightly disgruntled youth workers and research team tried to encourage them. They held firm, like a Roman testudo, and showed no desire whatsoever even to begin to experiment with the paints.

After a while, one of the lead youth workers, who was clearly a little embarrassed by how things hadn't gone to plan, gave up and left the paints, the paper and the bemused artist in the room, giving us all permission to go and do something else for the remainder of the session. At some point, Adil and I got talking again, and, just before it was time to go home, he pulled me back towards the abandoned spray-paints and paper. He picked up a can of purple paint and started to spray something that looked very elementary onto a piece of paper. He kept looking at me to see if I'd worked out what it was. At first, I thought it was a deformed tree, or a lollipop, and I ventured a guess. I took the fact that he simply carried on painting as evidence of the fact that I'd guessed wrong. Then I realized that it wasn't a tree, or a lollipop, but a cricket bat! It wasn't the most eloquently painted cricket bat in the world, but I could see very clearly that it was a cricket bat.

'Cricket!' I exclaimed, as though we were playing charades, and he suddenly looked at me and smiled as brightly as I'd seen him smile up to that point. His eyes lit up.

'Yes! Cricket!' he replied.

At the workshop the following week, the boys didn't even bother to turn up. A disgruntled football coach put his equipment back into the trunk of his car and bemoaned the fact that he'd made 'all that effort for nothing'. The same happened again with the rock-climbing session, and again with the tennis. Most of them did, however, turn up the following week, when someone presented a slide show about nature and wildlife. They seemed to like talking about how the mountains were similar to the mountains in their home countries. But, for the most part, they were letting us know, by voting with their feet, that this part of the project was, to put it bluntly, a dismal failure.

The photography session seemed to get their attention. They were excited by the fact that they were each gifted a digital camera to do with as they wished. We asked them to take photographs of anything that captured their interest and to build up a personal collection that represented 'them'. Later, they would build a collage that reflected who they were, using a selection of their own pictures. The room was buzzing that evening, in stark contrast to the flat atmosphere that had characterized it on that first week with the spray-paints. Towards the end of the session, Adil and some of the other Pashto-speaking boys came up to us and asked if we could finish the session early so they could show us something. The youth workers agreed, and we found ourselves bundled into a couple of cars as the boys directed us across the city. We drove through heavy traffic, and they directed us to the car park of a leisure centre in a rundown area.

'Cricket!' Adil said to me, and smiled broadly.

So, we found ourselves visiting a street cricket project in a large sports hall that seemed to be *the* place to go for anyone in the city who was looking to play cricket for free. The boys lit up and were clearly delighted to be there that evening. They whooped and howled with excitement and started enthusiastically demonstrating to each other their batting prowess and bowling action. Adil smiled at me and led me to the viewing area, where he told me we could watch them playing. Apparently, the British ruling classes attempted to transplant a cricketing culture into Afghanistan during the Anglo-Afghan Wars of 1839–42 and 1878–80. However, it is generally accepted that the sport really took hold when refugees living in Pakistan brought it back with them some 150 years later. Today, there are 330 clubs and thirty turf wickets in Afghanistan, new stadiums are under construction all the time, and the national team is thriving. Cricket is firmly a part of Afghan culture.[2]

As I watched Adil playing cricket that night, I was full of admiration for how talented he and the other Afghan boys were. They played with a skilful know-how that clearly impressed and bamboozled some of the other players and even the coaches. They batted gracefully and bowled aggressively, and they looked as though they were loving every minute of it. From time to time, Adil would look up at me when he hit a sublime reverse scoop, or an inside-out shot, or had taken another wicket with a reverse swing. As everyone applauded him, he smiled at me, and I smiled back. I felt like my presence mattered to him in the same way it had been important to my own son when I watched him play

Joseph in his first Nativity, or a wise man in his second, or a pirate, sheep or even a tree in subsequent school productions. I was always there, looking on and encouraging him. Adil gave me that look, a look that you just know reflects a feeling of comfort because someone is there to watch *you*, which somehow makes you feel like you matter – just a bit. What struck me most powerfully was the way Adil's entire demeanour and aura shifted that night. His escape from persecution had been a long, treacherous, lonely journey. But, in the sports hall, playing street cricket long into the night, he looked for the first time since I'd met him as though he belonged and as though he had found a sense of connection to something that felt like 'home' again.

The End of Hurdleditch Road

It's 1984. I'm five years old. I'm desperately trying to disguise the fact that I'm crying. I don't want the teacher or the other two children at my table to know that I'm distraught because I've now rubbed out the answer to the question in my maths book five times. In fact, I've rubbed out the answer so many times that the eraser has worn a hole in the page. I stare down at it, horrified at the fact that I've literally destroyed my maths book with my eraser. I brush away the offending bright pink rubber shavings with my sleeve. I don't understand where I'm going wrong. I've presented each attempt to Mrs Gritt, and each time she's sent me back to my table, instructing me to erase it, try again, and bring her the correct answer. I feel myself descending into panic. I feel ashamed, incompetent and under pressure.

Realizing that the rectangular answer box for problem 2b on page seven of my maths book has worn away, I hastily hatch an escape plan. I ask Mrs Gritt if I can go to the toilet. The toilet is located in the cloakroom, where we all hang our coats and PE bags. The pegs have stickers above them with our names neatly written on in marker pen, in what seems to my five-year-old self to be the kind of incredibly neat handwriting that I should aspire to. There's a doorway at the far end of that cloakroom that opens out onto the playground. Mrs Gritt seems preoccupied fixing Steven Anderson's glasses with Sellotape, and she agrees to my request.

I don't go to the toilet. I grab my coat from my peg and I

make for the door. I'm out on the playground now, and I just need to make it past the windows of the other classrooms without being seen. Then, I'll be at the school gate, home free. The playground is empty. I creep round the corner and crawl on my hands and knees, like a cross between a small animal and a commando, underneath the windowsills of the other four classrooms, so that nobody can possibly see me. I walk down the path to the school gate – it's open, and I've escaped.

Hurdleditch Road suddenly looms before me, and I stand at the roadside, staring down the country lane. It's probably about half a mile long, but seems endless and daunting. I'm aware that I live somewhere beyond the end of that lane, but I haven't paid meticulous attention to exactly which route the school bus takes, and I know there's a main road out there that Mum always tells us is dangerous. I don't know it yet, but this will not be the last time I'll contemplate the mysteries beyond the end of Hurdleditch Road. Many years later, I will again sense the unknown at the end of that road and wonder about the perils that lie beyond it.

Suddenly, anxiety sets in and the relief associated with my successful escape plan dissipates. It's as though the fear of the escape outweighs the shame and incompetence I was feeling back in the classroom, and I'm caught between a rock and a hard place.

I re-evaluate, abort mission and make my way back along the path, crawling back under the windowsills, crossing the playground, entering the cloakroom, returning my coat to my peg and walking back into my classroom. Mrs Gritt hasn't noticed. She's still fixing Steven's glasses. I return to the shame and incompetence that, even as a five-year-old, I have hastily calculated is the lesser of two evils.

*

It would be Chris who would again arouse my interest in the mysteries at end of Hurdleditch Road. Chris was my uncle, Dad's youngest stepbrother. I didn't really know him, even though he lived no more than five miles away from our house for the duration of my childhood. 'Family' can be used to denote a broad spectrum of different sorts of relationships, ranging from deep and meaningful affectionate bonds to relatively meaningless obligations. Chris was part of the 'family' we all bundled into the car to visit every Christmas Eve and on special occasions. They were 'courtesy visits' that we fulfilled to satisfy some sort of unwritten rule that visiting 'family' is an important thing to do at Christmas and sometimes on birthdays too.

We would exchange gifts with Dad's side of the family, and our German 'Nana' would prepare the same array of bread, cheese, a variety of salami, German cookies that smelled of cinnamon and sugar, and a traditional cake like a *Weihnachtsstollen*. I would load my plate up with as many of the sweet, crumbly cookies as I could get away with, and I'd peel the peppery rind, too spicy for my undeveloped palate, from the salami, discard it and place the rindless meat on top of slices of bread that I liberally covered with butter. We'd mingle with relatives we didn't really know and try to make polite conversation with people who didn't really know us.

During these visits, my uncle rarely came out of his room. He was only about a decade older than us children, and we always wondered what he did in there. All we knew was that his room had a mysterious red light bulb, and occasionally, when the door was ajar, as you walked past his room to go to the toilet, you could see that he had model aeroplanes and fishing equipment inside. His room was a mystery to us, and so was he – our mysterious, hermit-like uncle. Dad never really talked about him either. He was about seventeen years younger than Dad – Nana had married again (Dad's father had died when he was a baby) and had two further children. Chris was the youngest by far, and, perhaps because of the large age gap or the complexities of stepfamily dynamics, they didn't seem particularly close.

My idea of my uncle, then, did not evolve out of an authentic relationship, but from snippets of information and facts that my young imagination must have stitched together to form a warped, and probably inaccurate, understanding of who he was. Mum used him as an exemplar of what we'd become if we elected to stay in our rooms when we had visitors, in the same way she used 'the boy who cried wolf' to discourage us from telling exaggerated tales just to get each other into trouble. 'Look, do you want to end up like *Chris*,' she would say, 'stuck up here in your bedroom, when you're in your twenties or thirties, scared to see anyone, antisocial, biting your nails?' As a shy, private child, I often preferred to run for the hills when my family were entertaining. But, as she said it, Mum would do an impression of a nervous, nail-biting, wide-eyed person that would have the desired effect of making you feel ashamed that you had ever even contemplated something as ludicrous as staying closeted away in your room while we were hosting guests.

I knew that Chris had never moved out of his parents' house, and he lived there through his twenties and thirties, in the same room, with the same red light bulb. I knew that he had left school at sixteen and had a job in a local factory that produced fibre-cement profiled sheeting for the roofs of a full range of agricultural buildings. I knew that he spent many of his evenings drinking in the Chequers with the locals and he also played for the pub football team. In these circles, a friend of mine told me, he was more affectionately known as 'Stoffy' – a nickname that was not as extravagant as it sounds, but simply an affectionate, playful revision of the second syllable of his full name (Christopher). One year, out of the blue, he bought my dad, my brother and I some really expensive fishing equipment for Christmas. It was completely out of character, and we never knew why he was so generous towards us that year. It made us pay him a little more attention, briefly. Then it was back to normal, with Chris largely trying to avoid us as much as we tried to avoid him. We never managed to catch any fish.

Chris never had a serious relationship, as far as we knew. But he did have a sexual affair with Mrs Barrett, who lived directly opposite our house, in number twenty-four. It was my sister – sitting behind the net curtains on the windowsill in our living room, chatting to her friend, Sharon, on the phone – who revealed it. We heard her shriek in excitement and urgently call us all to the window. Dad was at work – he wouldn't have approved – but my brother, Mum and I rushed to her side and peered through the net curtain as though we were watching a particularly engrossing episode of *Neighbours*. To add to the drama, my sister didn't put the phone down – rather, she narrated what was unfolding to her friend, so that Sharon could hear it in real time.

Mrs Barrett was well into her sixties, and she was married to Mr Barrett, a thin, spindly, balding and bearded man, who looked as though he worked as an accountant. He would leave and return at the same time every day. But, on that day, for some reason, he came home early. He'd parked up on the drive and stepped out of the car, closing the driver's-side door behind him, just as he did every day. Then he'd opened the rear door of the car, taking out his briefcase and folding his raincoat across his forearm, before closing the car door, locking the car and purposefully walking towards his front door.

As she was chatting, my sister had casually observed Mr Barrett arriving home. Soon afterwards, the bedroom window had opened and Chris had climbed out, half-dressed and looking incredibly sheepish. At which point my sister had squealed. We then all watched him sneak onto the driveway, trying desperately to pull up his jeans, quietly open the boot of Mrs Barrett's Peugeot 205, climb inside, and close it behind him with such gentleness that it didn't make a sound. Just as he'd done so, Mr and Mrs Barrett returned to the front door. She looked dishevelled, panicked, and was wearing her bright pink dressing gown. Mr Barrett looked furious. He looked up and down the road for the 'other man' and, when he couldn't spot him, had a brief argument with his wife, before jumping into his own car and screeching off down the road. Mrs Barrett made sure that her husband had driven well out of sight before she hurriedly dressed herself, then drove my uncle away, still half-dressed in the boot of her car. According to the rumours that went round the village, their affair ended shortly after that.

As we grew up and changed, it seemed Chris didn't. He continued to live with his parents, and he stayed in his room every Christmas Eve, without fail. The red light bulb never went out, and we caught only rare glimpses of him. He seemed like a lonely figure to us, but continued to be a regular part of the pub football team and was a regular presence in the Chequers. To them, perhaps, he was the life and soul of the party.

Oddly, I can remember what I was wearing when he died. I would have been in my late teens and was sporting a pair of sleek black Nike Air trainers with a luminous pink swoosh down the side. I was utterly obsessed with Nike Airs and

Reebok Pumps in my teens, and I spent all of my paper-round earnings on that sort of footwear. At £6.50 a week, it took many months before I earned enough money for a top-of-the-range pair of trainers. I was also wearing a Cambridge United football shirt with the name of their sponsor, Fujitsu, advertised on the front, and a pair of adidas jogging bottoms with curious press studs up the side of each leg that enabled you to take them off by ripping them apart. These were the days before athleisure as standard issue. I liked running and I ran around the country lanes and woods that surrounded our home in rural Cambridgeshire.

I got the impression Chris also liked those lanes and woods, because I would often bump into him while running. I encountered him so regularly that he became more than just someone I noted but quickly forgot within a few seconds of our paths crossing. After a while, I started to think about him as I ran, hazarding guesses and making hypotheses about his walking route and daily routine. It seemed to me that he walked the very same route every day, a lengthy combination of country roads, hills, woodland and the grounds of a nearby National Trust estate, which I calculated must have been a good seven miles. He seemed to be a creature of habit and it must have taken him a few hours to complete his daily circuit. I had decided that he probably stopped at the Chequers halfway through his walk, as he always seemed to come from Hurdleditch Road. I noted that he wore the same clothes every day: a pair of tight, snow-washed jeans that were slightly too short for his lanky legs, a dark-green parker coat that he always wore with the hood up, and surprisingly clean, white high-top trainers, manufactured by Hi-Tec.

He walked quickly and purposefully, and we always acknowledged each other as our paths crossed. We never actually spoke, however, other than a quick 'Hi', 'All right?' or

'How's it going?' accompanied by a nod and some very brief eye contact. I think I saw more of Chris during that time than I ever had in my life. For a while, he was a regular feature of my runs, like the beautiful old oak, my favourite tree-lined hill or the place in the grounds of the National Trust estate where I would sit and contemplate life.

On that day, when our paths crossed, there was something about the eye contact that was different. You wouldn't notice it unless you watched the moment back on tape and I talked you through it, play by play. If I could pause life at exactly 11.53 a.m. on 14 November 2005, you'd see me in my running gear, crossing paths with my uncle, in his usual walking attire, right at the end of Hurdleditch Road, just off the A603, where a quiet lane leads down to the woodlands that surround the National Trust estate. If you analysed it carefully, you'd notice that he held my gaze for much, much longer than usual that day. He actually looked into my eyes – in a way that he had never done – and I looked into his. I remember noticing how beautiful his blue eyes were. Of course, we didn't speak – other than the usual 'Hi' – but the interaction was markedly different. For a split second, our souls met, and I saw him, and he saw me. I will never forget those few seconds of unbroken eye contact with an uncle I never really knew. At the time, I don't think I recognized the vulnerability and desperation in his gaze. I sometimes feel frustrated at my younger self. Maybe I should have seen it, maybe I missed a chance in that split-second to reach out to him, to help him, to connect to him. I feel as though a more mature version of myself might have recognized how his eyes obliquely conveyed a sense that he had had enough of living.

There were police helicopters all around the National Trust estate, later that week. They chuffed around like big bumblebees looking for something that only they knew they were looking for. My mum put the phone down and I noticed that she was crying and unusually distressed, even for Mum. They'd found him swinging from the bough of a tree in the woods that lined the National Trust estate. I think I was the last person he'd had any sort of human contact with. He left a suicide note for his mother that said he didn't want to live any longer, that he was deeply lonely, depressed and could not find a reason to exist. I wondered how he must have felt as he took that fateful last walk. Was he afraid? Did he contemplate the fact that this was to be the very last time he'd walk along the lanes, through the fields and down Hurdleditch Road, on to meet death? Did he think about Mrs Barrett? Did he have second thoughts? There is a paper, published in the *Journal of Forensic Sciences*, which documents the agonal sequences of a case in which a suicidal man had for some reason filmed his own hanging. It took thirteen seconds for him to become unconscious, one minute and thirty-eight seconds for him to lose muscle tone, and four minutes and ten seconds for all muscle movement to cease.[3]

On the day of the funeral, I pulled into the car park of the crematorium and noticed that Dad had arrived too. It would be that very same crematorium in which I would struggle through Dad's own funeral, seventeen years later. But he was younger then and not yet immobile and decrepit. He looked socially uncomfortable, and was wearing a suit and a pair of black rubber Crocs on his feet. Dad told me, as we waited to go inside the crematorium, that he had a pair of black Crocs reserved especially for funerals, a pair of white ones for weddings, and various other colours to cover almost every occasion. Buying Crocs in bulk in this way meant that he could avoid shopping for footwear on multiple occasions and could capitalize on what he called a 'good deal'. I remember listening to this matter-of-fact explanation and looking into his eyes, scrutinizing his every move, looking for a sign that he felt something about his brother's tragic suicide – but, as usual, he kept his cards close to his chest.

There are so many complexities and dimensions of loneliness, disconnection or confusion that colour the dynamic of the relationship between the suicide and the remaining survivors. The psychologist, Allen Battle, identified that survivors often interpret what the suicide victim was saying in complex and painful ways. 'When the suicide says, "I can't handle the problem"', he writes, 'they are also saying "you can't handle the problem either".' He continues, 'For some survivors, the suicide is saying "My death is preferable to my trying to work out my problems with you or through you; therefore, you and I are terribly distant."'[4]

I wondered whether Dad felt any of these things, but I didn't know how to ask him.

Loneliness was a part of my uncle's story and of his death. It's hard to argue with that when someone uses the word 'lonely' in a suicide note. But I never heard his story as he would have chosen to tell it, and I never really knew him. Psychiatrists from the University of Leuven, in Belgium, listened to the stories of adults who had attempted suicide. They wanted to hear first-hand about the process and experiences that precede people's suicide attempts. One of the major themes to emerge was loneliness, feeling alone in the world after a significant loss, helplessly drifting further and further out of touch with the world, being unable to let others in, or suffering unfulfilling, non-reciprocal relationships. The participants described intense experiences of loneliness that were frequently a major factor in their decision to take their own lives.[5]

There is a difference between 'dying alone' and 'dying lonely'. According to Holly Nelson-Becker and Christina Victor from London's Brunel University, 'ultimately, everyone "dies alone" since we go through that door by ourselves'.[6] However, the process of dying itself need not *feel* lonely, even if we do have to walk through that door alone. Dying alone, like living alone, does not imply that we will necessarily *feel* lonely when we die – but something tells me my uncle did.

Snow White's Cottage

When I arrived for my interview with Veronica, I drove into a neat and tidy gated retirement community, where the houses and streets were well manicured and uncluttered. The developer had done a good job of creating a sense of architectural harmony while still offering consumer choice in the form of an array of different sized and styled properties. Veronica's house was one of the smallest, with two bedrooms and a neat back garden. She lived there with Philip, her husband, who had developed early-onset dementia at the age of fifty. She had been caring for him ever since.

I immediately warmed to Veronica; I had liked how reflective and thoughtful she was when we talked on the phone. She was a stout, short woman, with a slightly unkempt, grey bob cut, wearing a baggy woolly jumper and a pair of black trousers. She was Dutch and had retained her strong accent, as well as the admirable non-British tendency to say exactly what she felt or thought, rather than skirting around a point politely. It was clear to me that she had been waiting eagerly for our conversation. Philip was being taken care of for the afternoon by a friend, and there was a tea tray carefully laid out for us, with spoons, sugar and a jug of milk. Two armchairs had been positioned side by side in the living room, facing a beautiful walnut grandfather clock whose tick would provide a backing track for our conversation. She had also made extensive notes about her life on an A4 pad, which she consulted diligently as we talked.

Veronica had one parental bond that she had experienced as warm and tender, but the other, she told me, could feel cold, rejecting and wounding. 'My father was warm. He was just a big, beautiful bear. But my mother wasn't cuddly at all. He was so warm, very shy, but affectionate, and we later developed a wonderful intellectual rapport.'

She had grown up in a small village during the German occupation of the Netherlands in the Second World War. Her father had been the village doctor, and her mother a nurse. She showed me a photograph, which she pulled out of a green A4 plastic wallet that looked as though it had been carefully prepared, filled with useful artefacts and resources for our conversation. He was a very tall man, wearing a suit and round, wire-rimmed glasses. He looked kind and gentle as he stared into the camera, leaning forwards, with one hand gently placed on his daughter's shoulder. Her mother looked younger and had a notably more serious expression.

'She was dutiful, willing to help others but not the family,' Veronica told me, pointing at her mother. 'She hated me. She mistrusted me. She was . . . not normal.'

I was curious to know what she meant by 'not normal', and I asked if she would mind elaborating. Veronica said she had a memory that would help me understand. Her memory was a recollection of a maternal relationship that had perplexed and challenged her in equal measure.

'We lived in the old vicarage,' she explained. 'It was this fantastic house, with a long driveway and big rooms.' On the day in question, she told me, she had been playing in the bath with her brother. She thought that she would have been about three years old, which would have made her brother around four years old. Their mother, she remembered, had been playing with them, scrubbing them down in the tub and engaging with them in a way that felt safe and normal. Some time passed, and, as Veronica was playing, it suddenly dawned on her that her mother wasn't there. She experienced the feeling of mild but rising panic young children get when they aren't sure of their caregiver's whereabouts, but haven't yet logged the absence as a full-blown emergency.

'I got out of the bath and instinctively ran to the window,' she explained. 'I saw my mother cycling away – she had forgotten us, completely forgotten us. She didn't come back until very late that night and she didn't even tell us she was going. She just . . . left us.'

I asked Veronica if she could remember how she had felt as a three-year-old, standing at the bathroom window, dripping wet and naked, alone with her brother in the house.

'Well, I was devastated,' she replied. 'I felt so alone. I cried and I cried. My cries reflected the terror of abandonment. I remember I crawled into my bed and hid under the blankets. I couldn't understand how my mother could just forget about us. It was like she'd suddenly forgotten she had children. Much, much later, I heard my father come home. He came into my room and whispered, "You were very brave, how good of you to go to bed." I don't know what my brother did, after she left.'

Veronica had experienced the barrage of emotion that hits you as a child when a caregiver you instinctively trusted to keep you safe and provide nurturance abandons or rejects you in a way that feels cruel, insensitive or unpredictable. You are suddenly adrift. You feel completely unseen, unimportant and forgotten. Such lonely experiences in childhood are frequently the prototype for the longer-term landscape. Veronica went on to tell me the story of a maternal relationship that seemed to repeat a simple pattern: she would reach out to her mother, or trust in her, only to be wounded by savage, unpredictable, painful and confusing responses that invariably left her panicked, bewildered and feeling invisible – just like the early experience of abandonment in the bathroom.

'The worst event of my life happened when I was eight,' she told me. 'My mother had to undergo all sorts of operations in hospital. She stayed there for about three weeks.' She paused, as the grandfather clock ticked on. 'During this time, I was allowed to sleep in my father's bed. I was so happy, because I was never allowed to sleep in their bed! And I so desperately wanted to feel safe, warm and secure. It was such a very happy time, because my father was just a big, loving body to be near. And I wasn't used to much cuddling, so it was heaven,' she said excitedly.

'When I knew that my mother was coming back from hospital, I wrote her a little note,' she continued. 'It said, in eight-year-old writing, "Mother, I hope you are getting better. I'm so enjoying sleeping in your bed – from now on, you can have my bed!"'

The letter, she told me, enraged her mother, who responded by constructing a story that her husband had sexually abused their daughter while she was hospitalized. On her return, she furiously berated Veronica and her father for a series of events that Veronica assured me never happened.

'My mother had all sorts of angry outbursts after that,' she remembered. 'She was utterly convinced that my father had done all sorts of terrible things to me – which he hadn't – and she was furious. It must have been horrendous for my father too, because I'm pretty sure he would have denied having done anything wrong – but how do you prove that?' she asked incredulously. 'From that moment, I have no doubt that my mother hated me. I'm certain that her objective was to sort of "delete me" from the family. And the rumour certainly caused Father to distance himself from me, to defend himself from the shame of the allegations. They both completely isolated me after that. I melted away into the background of the family and I genuinely don't think either of them noticed or cared whether I existed or not.'

Veronica seemed bewildered, as though she herself couldn't make sense of the story she was telling me, even all these years later. 'I felt so alone,' she continued. 'Around that time, at school, I met this old lady, a very old lady, who somehow had heard something about me not being happy at home. The lady said, "Oh, I've got this little cottage in the woods – you can have a key and escape there whenever you want to!" That's what she told me. It was like she knew I was suffering and wanted to help me escape my troubles, escape the suffering. So, I did – for months on end, I would just disappear and stay on my own in this very primitive little cottage, deep in the woods.'

Veronica told me she lived alone in the cottage as a little girl for long periods of time. Nobody at home seemed to care, and she survived by stealing scraps of food from the house and taking them to the cottage.

'Oh, yes, I'm not sure they even noticed I was gone,' she remembered. 'I was woken up by the birds every morning, there was no electricity and the water came out of a pump.'

I remembered a cheap Disney picture book my grandparents had bought us from a car-boot sale. It was a slightly tarnished copy of *Snow White and the Seven Dwarfs*. In the book, Snow White's stepmother, the wicked queen, enlists a woodsman to murder her, but he cannot commit the act and exhorts Snow White to escape into the forest. Deep in the woods, she stumbles upon an apparently deserted cottage, home to the seven dwarfs, where she finds refuge. I liked looking at the picture of Snow White on the front cover. She was sitting in a very comfy-looking wooden bed, under a beautiful patchwork quilt, the bedroom window was open and I always imagined that it was morning, because the sun was shining, the sky was blue and the forest outside seemed alive and awake. Snow White was stretching, her arms were out in front of her, her head thrown back. There were three beautiful bluebirds, which I imagined had entered through the open window, flying around her head and chirping. A procession of musical notes, denoting song, seemed to come from their beaks. I felt as though she had found sanctuary in the forest when the rest of the world had forgotten her.

Three hours later, I looked at the clock and realized how long Veronica and I had been talking. The grandfather clock ticked on, and so did Veronica – I got the impression she could have talked all night. She told me that she also had a younger sister, Hilda, whom she loved very much. She spent much of her childhood caring for Hilda and took great pride in the fact that she had been a mother figure to the younger girl. When she grew up, Hilda went to live in France, not far from Paris. Apparently, she was a bit of a wild, troubled soul, always searching for something that she never quite found. Hilda was a sort of wandering artist, and she had a string of inappropriate boyfriends and did crazy things like squatting in an abandoned railway signal box, which she covered with mandalas and boho prints. Sadly, as a young adult, Hilda developed a melanoma that was left untreated and metastasized.

'She eventually had chemotherapy,' Veronica told me matter-of-factly. 'But it was far too late to save her. She was enormously swollen, her head was all big and puffy, and she lost her hair. She had such beautiful hair.'

Hilda died in an ill-equipped hospice in rural France. Veronica told me that she couldn't stand the thought of being so far away from her little sister as she died. 'So, that next morning, I went to my personnel manager in Holland and said, "Sorry, you can sack me, but I must go and sit beside my sister until she dies." And that is what I did.'

Hilda died just hours after Veronica's arrival – but not without further anguish.

'My sister was in so much pain,' she sighed. 'So, I said to this doctor, "She is suffering so much! Can't you do some-thing?" The doctor, who was also Dutch, replied, "We are both from Holland, we don't let people suffer in the last stage of life. Don't worry."

'Well, I hadn't thought about euthanasia or anything, but she was dying and suffering – do you have to let people go on in that sort of pain?' Veronica reflected. 'The doctor then increased the morphine with my consent, which had the effect of organ failure. And she died.'

Veronica returned to Holland to deliver the news of Hil-da's death. Her father had long since died and her mother was fading from a long-term terminal illness that had forced her into hospice care. When she informed her mother that Hilda had died, Veronica hoped somewhere inside that it might create one last opportunity for them to bond through grief. Instead, as she sat at her mother's bedside, the old woman opened her eyes, looked at her coldly and delivered these final words: 'I am so disappointed in you. You let them kill her and I'll never forgive you for that. Now, you'll pay for it.'

At this point, Veronica wept.

'My mother then closed her eyes and her mouth. She was a very determined woman. And, from then on, it was impos-sible to put anything into her – not food nor water. She refused the lot,' she said tearfully. 'I had to make the decision, with the doctors, not to force-feed her. And, ten days after my sister died, my mother died too.'

Veronica told me that her mother's death felt familiar. It repeated a toxic pattern that had characterized their relationship throughout her life.

'I have never understood why,' she reflected, wiping the tears from her eyes with a tissue, 'but my mother repeatedly abandoned me throughout my life, and she seemed to have this pathological need to punish me by refusing to acknowledge me, refusing to *see* me. There is nothing more painful than feeling as though you are unseen by your mother.'

After her mother's death, Veronica was again left alone, drowning in a pool of shame, guilt, anger, frustration and self-loathing. In her childhood, Veronica had managed to get away from it all, temporarily, to the cottage in the woods. Metaphorically speaking, even now, at the end of her life, she was still seeking psychological, emotional and spiritual refuge.

My colleague and friend, Professor Malcolm Johnson, visiting professor of gerontology and end-of-life care at the University of Bath, first introduced me to the concept of biographical pain during a conversation we shared over lunch.[7] We had been judged a good academic match by a mutual acquaintance and we'd arranged to meet in the university refectory. The lunchtime rush was over, and it was my favourite time of day for a meeting. Only a few small congregations of graduate students and academics remained, and the tables were mostly empty. From the window, you can see the hustle and bustle of the campus below and you appreciate that the university really does feel like a world within a world. That day, Malcolm spoke with a calm and assured sense of confidence in his ideas about biographical pain.

According to Malcolm, biographical pain is a unique form

of psychological and spiritual suffering in older people that involves profoundly painful recollection and reliving of experienced wrongs, self-promises or regretted actions, often dealt with in the face of finitude. In other words, there is something particularly unique about the kind of suffering we experience when nearing the end of our lives, looking back over unhealed wounds, unresolved conflicts and various regrets or unfulfilled needs that so often litter the landscape of a life lived. For many older people, this sort of biographical pain can bleed into the time and space that opens up before us, in ways that life doesn't permit in the hustle and bustle of younger adulthood. In the twilight of life, a circus of pain, regret and unresolved wounds had undoubtedly caught up with Veronica.

Veronica told me that, around the time she lived in the little cottage in the woods, she found a friend in the most unlikely of places. During the war, her village was occupied by the German invaders, and a troop of soldiers moved in, taking over buildings and ensuring that the local population was under control.

'You had to negotiate with them, you had to survive,' she explained. 'This German officer marched up and claimed our house, but my dad took him up to the attic and managed to make him step on a non-insulated wire, so he got an electric shock. He jumped in the air, and that seemed to be enough to convince him that we could continue to live in part of our house, and the soldiers, well, they would live in the rest and occupy the outbuildings in the garden.

'They just claimed part of the house and the outbuildings and laid out their mattresses on the floor,' she continued. 'And I remember walking around my house and realizing that we were about to be roommates with a bunch of soldiers that my parents, village and entire nation hated with a passion.

'And so, this group of young men essentially just moved in. They were the youngest of the young – some may have been no more than fifteen years old. The Germans were running out of soldiers at this point.'

Though her parents had forbidden her to interact with the enemy, Veronica formed an unlikely connection with Max, a young German soldier, whom she described with affection. 'I was only a small child, but I loved him so much. He was blonde, always cheerful, and would pick me up, swing me round and cuddle me, like the loving big brother I never had, and I loved that,' she said, with a smile on her face. 'I have told you already, my mother wasn't cuddly at all, and she and my father had completely distanced themselves from me. I was lonely and Max was my knight in shining armour.'

She reached into the green plastic folder again and showed me a picture of herself at the time – a small girl, with dark, neatly plaited hair, sitting at her school desk, holding a pen, looking into the camera and half smiling.

'I remember standing and looking out for my hero, my German friend, Max, and hoping beyond hope that he would swirl me round on the area where they marched and shouted,' she continued.

One day, as she sat like a lost puppy outside the soldiers' room, listening to their laughter and cheers, she noticed a pool of thick, sticky liquid oozing out from under the door and slowly trickling into the corridor. Instinctively, she tasted it, dabbing her fingers in it, sampling it like a lobster bisque.

'It tasted horrible!' she remembered. 'It was blood from some animal they were slaughtering on the table. I was flabbergasted. I had seen animals that had been killed and hung on a ladder, and I knew that they bled. But that was not a very kind thing to do! How could my Max be involved in such a thing? Such a very bad thing!' She paused. 'You see, I was always waiting for anyone I got close with to disappear on me, turn into a monster, reveal themselves to be a mirage, suddenly stop seeing me – as though either I, or they, or the relationship we shared had all been a trick.'

There is a loneliness that arises from the doubt and lack of trust that understandably develop when life teaches us that intimate relationships have the capacity to wound us savagely, as though they have, quite unpredictably and unexpectedly, turned into a rabid dog.

Beyond Sheremetyevo

In Moscow, I learned that my friends and I all felt lonely, disconnected from the world, and were longing for some sort of panacea. We had all been compelled to escape the fact that we couldn't find what we were looking for at home, and hoped for some sort of utopia on the other side of Sheremetyevo airport. I imagine us as severed electricity cables, like the ones you sometimes see in children's cartoons, sparking and thrashing around like snakes, looking for something to plug ourselves into. TEFL (Teaching English as a Foreign Language) offered the perfect opportunity for young, reasonably educated, native English speakers to do a quick qualification, stick a pin in a map and get the hell out of Dodge.

And the nice thing about it was that you could have your quarter-life crisis under the guise of having an adventure abroad, strengthening your CV or taking a gap year. It placed an acceptable, even desirable, facade over a period of your life that could just as easily have seen you end up a mental-health outpatient. Years later, when people asked you what you did in your early twenties, you could choose to narrate that troubled part of your life truthfully – admitting that 90 per cent of us were terrified and adrift, desperately looking for or running away from something – or, if you were too ashamed to tell it like that, you'd always have the luxury of making yourself sound like a well-rounded human being who'd recognized and latched on to a valuable opportunity to develop cultural awareness and independence.

We drove through the chaotic streets of Moscow, not really having any idea where we were headed. Lena told us that we should not go out – *at all* – over the weekend, because we did not have our official registration documents yet and would be arrested if the police stopped us – which, she told us, was not uncommon.

I remember, on that journey through Moscow, how I experienced the very same feeling I'd had on my first day of secondary school, travelling to Bassingbourn Village College on the 1970s school bus operated by the local bus firm, Kenzie's, and driven by Stephen Burford's dad. I sat timidly and watched, wide-eyed, while the older children on the bus shouted, laughed, teased each other and generally acted boisterously, like a troop of chimps. I had my timetable for the day and I knew my form tutor would be someone called Mrs Billings, but I felt as though I was driving into the unknown, and I was afraid. It wasn't a dissimilar feeling ten years later, in Moscow. Lena gave me a piece of paper with the school's address scrawled on it, a Metro pass valid for ten journeys, a map of the Moscow Metro and the address of the apartment that would be my home for the foreseeable future. I felt even lonelier when I realized that Zeek, the only person in Russia to whom I had any sort of connection in that moment, would be living in a different district entirely, which we worked out was a minimum of twenty Metro stops away.

In my district, everything looked the same. It was, Lena told me matter-of-factly, one of Moscow's more deprived areas. I could see nothing but vast rows of ugly grey high-rise blocks of Soviet-era housing, which, like Igor, were austere and unwelcoming, an endless row of giant hostile ogres. We drove up to my apartment block and I immediately noted the graffitied Russian messages that defaced the door of the building. The door was broken and no longer served a purpose, because it neither locked nor shut properly. The lift, also heavily graffitied, filthy and stinking of urine, groaned its way into action, and felt as though it might give out at any second, plummeting us to our deaths. But we made it to the thirteenth floor and, from her handbag, Lena produced the keys to my apartment. She unlocked two heavy-duty iron doors, which looked as though they would be suitable for a high-security prison, and slammed them shut behind us as we went inside. I was relieved the doors were so robust; it made me feel safer.

And, suddenly, there we were, in an apartment that looked like the set of a cheap 1970s porn movie. I had a small, dirty kitchen, the floor of which was covered with a cheap orange lino that was peeling away at the edges. I didn't see them immediately, but there were cockroaches in the kitchen. Other teachers later informed me this was the norm rather than the exception. Apparently, two young American women had arrived at their apartment in the Dinamo area to be greeted by a pair of large black rats in the bath, so it could have been worse. The living room was garish, to say the least; a pair of dirty net curtains covered the doorway which led on to a small balcony. My bedroom was bare, apart from a small, uncomfortable single bed and a cheaply made wardrobe. The bathroom was the most unpleasant room of all – dirty, tired and unsanitary. I did, however, spot an old washing machine in the bathroom, which Lena informed me was a rarity, as most teachers had to wash their clothes in the tub. It worked, too.

Before she left, Lena also told me that there would be no hot water for a few months. I had arrived at the beginning of the annual two-month hot-water outage, which enabled the authorities to conduct essential maintenance work on the district's plumbing and heating system. She showed me a carton of milk, a loaf of bread and a block of cheese in my dilapidated refrigerator. It was to keep me going over the weekend, as I should, she reminded me, avoid going out on the street. She informed me that the school would deduct the cost of these groceries from my first month's salary. With that, she left to go back to her, I assumed, much nicer life.

Then, I was alone, on the thirteenth floor of a dismal apartment block, in a rundown district somewhere in southern Moscow. That night, I ventured onto my balcony and surveyed the view. I saw nothing but endless rows of the same grim apartment blocks looming out of the darkness. There wasn't much in the way of street lighting, but I could hear the endless hum of the Moscow traffic, dogs barking, people shouting, groups of drunken young men laughing and joking in a language I didn't understand. Everything felt alien, unfamiliar and threatening. I felt like an alien. As I looked out over Moscow's immensity, I was simultaneously exhilarated and more alone than I had ever felt.

I never really connected with the sex, drugs and rock 'n' roll side of Zeek. I tolerated it, but it wasn't really me. He pressured me into the Moscow club and bar scene from the get-go. He knew we were supposed to stay home that first weekend, but he called me the very next day.

'We won't get caught by the cops. You just have to be savvy, avoid them like the plague and, if they do stop you, just be ready to pay them a bribe,' he explained. It was as if he'd been doing this his entire life. 'My friend, Jake, back in New York, has given me a list of the coolest bars. So, let's go hit some – tonight. What do you say?'

And so, I found myself in a smoky, noisy, crowded bar somewhere in the centre of Moscow, slowly drinking one bottle of Baltika for every three bottles Zeek consumed. I watched him bopping his head and tapping his foot to the music, taking long drags of his cigarette and randomly speaking pidgin Russian to various scantily dressed women who caught his eye. He seemed genuinely at home in this environment, but all I could think about was getting back to the relative safety of my unwelcoming apartment, very much the lesser of two evils. I remember looking at Zeek as though I was observing a different species. That's how I used to feel when Dad took me to the local pub for a drink. I'd watch him revelling in laughter with the other barflies, holding court, downing endless pints of Guinness, until someone belatedly suggested he'd 'had a skinful' and it was time to go home.

I felt that I should make sure Zeek got home OK that night, because he was completely out of it. He had washed down the Baltika with multiple shots of vodka, encouraged by Sergei and Roman, two random Russian guys we'd met at the bar. I finally watched him stumble into his apartment block at midnight and made my way back to the Metro. This was how Zeek spent those first two years in Moscow. There were times when he'd make it back home and times when he wouldn't. He'd occasionally turn up for work with black eyes and bruised ribs, having passed out on the way home and been mugged by the gangs of skinheads who roamed the streets looking for easy prey. They'd take his phone, cash and wallet. He told me that the trick was to carry a fake wallet and only the bare minimum in cash. That way, if you were mugged, you didn't lose anything particularly important.

There was another side to Zeek, though – a more vulnerable, open, thoughtful side that he showed me from time to time. I tolerated Party Zeek because I always sensed there was more to him than that; when the other Zeek emerged, it was worth the wait.

One winter evening, we were walking home from the school, through Red Square, both sporting long, warm

Russian-style trench coats we'd picked up at a Moscow market to cope with the freezing temperatures (Zeek had heard about the market from one of his Russian friends). He suddenly stopped and suggested we sit down on a bench that offered a beautiful view of St Basil's Cathedral. In that moment, for whatever reason, staring at the multi-coloured onions that top the cathedral's towers and form a riot of beautiful colours and shapes, he opened up. He told me that his mum had died when he was ten and his dad had brought him up. He didn't feel particularly close to his dad and had never felt that he'd wanted him around after his mum died.

'To be honest,' he told me, 'I don't think I've ever found anyone I feel close to in the world, since Mom died. I feel as though I've been lost ever since, wandering around searching for something, and always in a little bit of pain. I've never found the sense of belonging I had when Mom was alive.'

Slowly, I became Zeek's confidant. He quickly found more suitable, skilful wingmen for his forays into Moscow's nightlife, but we would regularly meet to talk when he was sober and needed a different kind of companion and conversation.

Zeek and I were sitting on the side of a dirty road, staring at some of the ugly high-rise apartment blocks in his district. It was a hot day, and he'd bought us both a cold beer from one of the kiosks; we'd found a small amount of shade, provided by a skinny tree that looked half dead from the severe pollution, and settled down under it to drink our beer. I noticed a rat scurrying along the curb on the other side of the road. It ran towards a discarded sack of rubbish and disappeared.

It was at some point during that conversation that he told me about the Hungry Duck. The Hungry Duck was an iconic representation of Moscow's hedonism, a bar renowned for its rampant sexual antics, erotic strip shows, violence, wildness and debauchery. It was closed down by the state in the nineties, after complaints from members of the Russian Duma, but had reopened shortly afterwards. It was located near to Kuznetsky Most Metro station and was more commonly known by Muscovites as the Duck. Unsurprisingly, it was the venue for Zeek's birthday celebration that weekend and he made it abundantly clear he expected me to attend.

'It's gonna be a blast, dude,' he told me excitedly. 'Chicks, alcohol, sex and a whole lot of fun!' He smiled and I could see that he was genuinely excited about the prospect.

For his sake, I tried to match his enthusiasm, but, inside, I didn't get it. I understand excitement, of course – that's how I feel ahead of a visit to a reasonably empty library, an afternoon reading, a quiet walk in the mountains, or a flat-white coffee in a tranquil cafe. But I was, in no uncertain terms, dreading the excursion to the Duck.

We gathered in Zeek's apartment on the night in question. His birthday wish was that we'd all get 'totally wasted', then make our way to the Duck later in the evening. We were accompanied by Mike, Zeek's flatmate from Charleston, South Carolina, who was taking a break from his boyfriend for a year while they worked out their differences, and Wade, another of his drinking buddies whom I didn't know well. Mike looked a bit like Clark Kent, and Wade looked like a stereotype of a US college jock. I simply couldn't handle the amount of vodka they had lined up to drink before we left. I managed one, maybe two shots, and then resorted to secretly tipping them into plant pots while the others went into the kitchen to roll a joint or get more alcohol. By the time we left, Zeek's first birthday wish had been accomplished – or very nearly – as everyone, apart from me, was suitably drunk.

When we arrived at the club, the security guards and a

large gang of other men, whose role I could not decipher, were gathered around a reception kiosk, drinking beer in a masculine huddle. They looked like a gathering of muscular wildebeest in suits. They mocked us when we handed them our entrance fees, on account of the fact that we were all a little cautious and protective of our wallets as we took out the roubles to pay. We all sort of turned away from the crowd of men as we took out our money, because we had grown accustomed to being mugged and had developed a set of protective behavioural mechanisms. We hoped shielding our wallets would mitigate the risk. The large, bulky security guards laughed at us, imitating the way we had protected our wallets and clearly insinuating that we were a little pathetic for doing so. I imagined they would probably have been more impressed had we each been a little more 'mafioso', and taken a huge wad of 1,000-rouble notes from our hip, openly flashed it around, nonchalantly tossed them a few and told them to keep the change. Not even a drunk Zeek could pull that off.

Entering the Duck pretty much confirmed everything I'd feared. The music was too loud, the beat was too fast, the energy too manic, the lighting too psychedelic and the people too many and too much. I was overwhelmed in a matter of minutes. Zeek and the others, it seemed, were in their element. They were energized, alive, and immediately plugged themselves into the atmosphere, seemingly with no effort. I have always felt curious – jealous, perhaps – when people so easily feel at home in such an environment, because invariably I have always felt completely out of place.

We each bought a ridiculously overpriced drink, and that's when we parted company for the duration of the evening. They were participants. I felt more like a spectator. They went straight for the stage, right to the front, dancing merrily, raising their drinks aloft, randomly chatting to men and women who caught their eye. In contrast, I made straight for the edge of the room, where the wallflowers went – not that there were many. I found an empty table and sat with my drink, watching the crowd pulsing and moving like a school of brightly coloured tropical fish. I think my friends forgot about me from that point onwards.

When the strippers took to the stage, I worked out that there was an audience-participation component to some of the shows. The lights dimmed and a spotlight randomly circled the crowd, as though it were searching for someone in particular. Finally, it settled on Mike. I watched as two completely naked young female strippers dragged him onto the stage and began to undress him. At first, he protested and looked as though he might get away from them, but then he seemed to give up, a bit like helpless prey, resigned to its fate. They stripped him completely, using their hands and teeth, and a series of provocative and erotic sexual simulations followed. The crowd went wild. I could see Zeek and Wade right at the front, shouting at the top of their voices, whooping and pointing at Mike. When the track finished, the young women gave him his clothes back in a small bundle and allowed him to leave the stage.

What followed was a procession of strippers, invariably younger females doing duets or solo acts – 'ladies' night' was strictly reserved for Thursdays, when the strippers were exclusively male. I don't know how many strippers came and went while I sat there, on my own, nursing the same drink I'd bought when I arrived. It was all a bit of a blur. But, as various thoughts drifted in and out of my head, there was a moment when it all suddenly hit me, like a freight train, and I experienced a profound sense of awareness of just how inhumane it all felt to me, how disconnecting, how heartbreaking.

A young Kazakh girl had just started her act. She couldn't have been much older than twenty and you could see in her face that she was deeply unhappy. As she stood there, in white lace underwear and heels, it looked as though the over-the-top portrayal of excitement, happiness and phoney eroticism that the other performers had expertly presented to the crowd was beyond her. She seemed depressed, miserable, perhaps even trapped, as the increasingly intoxicated crowd of men near the front of the stage tried to put their hands on her body, or tuck 1,000-rouble notes into her underwear. I remembered a feeling of overwhelming sadness I had felt as a child when I'd been taken to a European circus and had seen how the big cats were made to perform. My nine-year-old blood had boiled at how wrong it all felt – the cruelty, the depravity. I couldn't understand how on earth anyone in the big top that night could possibly have believed that those animals *wanted* to be there, entertaining them.

At that moment, it was as though everything slowed down, including time itself. I noticed Zeek and Wade, positioned right at the front of the crowd, shouting, holding their glasses in the air, spilling their drinks like a couple of drunken Vikings. The whole crowd seemed riotous and out of control. Suddenly, I felt as though loneliness was all around me. We were all lonely. The overt objectification of the young Kazakh girl rendered her inhuman to the frenzied crowd and felt like an overt, oppressive form of loneliness. There was loneliness in the fact that I could not understand or relate to the horde of fellow men around me. I didn't understand them. I felt alienated from them. I'd heard the phrase 'alone in a crowd' and this was how I imagined it felt.

*

The other teachers who joined the ranks with Zeek and I also had their stories to tell. Jon was twenty-three years old. He stood no taller than five feet and didn't look old enough to have left school yet. He was scruffy and wore baggy ripped jeans and loose-fitting T-shirts that tended to swamp his slender frame. As it turned out, he'd grown up in Hertfordshire, close to my childhood home. We had a sort of intangible camaraderie that comes from growing up in the same region. There were local idiosyncrasies that slipped into our conversations, we knew the same places and shared a tacit cultural connection. Jon ended up in Moscow about three months after he had tried to kill himself by slitting his wrists in the bath with one of his sister's razors. His sister had discovered him in the tub before it was too late. His long-term girlfriend had left him shortly before his suicide attempt, he'd dropped out of university and generally felt like a failure in the eyes of his family. He was clearly depressed and said he didn't 'give a shit' where he was, so long as it was as far away as possible from Hertfordshire. Originally, he'd put his name down for a teaching contract in Azerbaijan, but the school had redeployed him to Moscow at the last minute because of staff shortages.

Kathy was a thirty-year-old from Massachusetts who suffered with anorexia. Her relationship with her abusive Moldovan boyfriend had ended in a flurry of violence when he struck her hard in the face and kicked her in the stomach during their final, heated argument, accusing her of being unfaithful with one of his friends. She came to Moscow to simultaneously escape the abuse and deal with the heartbreak she felt at losing someone she always insisted she still loved deeply. Some weekends, we shared long conversations into the early hours of the morning and fell asleep on the couch together.

Kirsty was a Canadian graduate of cultural studies who'd come to Moscow, she said, to escape the psychological and emotional torture of growing up in a 'religious cult'. She told me, over dinner one night, that she loved sex and her 'biggest turn-on' was being hit and generally being treated aggressively in the bedroom. She looked at me across the table through round, wire-framed glasses and told me that her father had physically punished her, and her sisters, for even mentioning sex. He believed they would go to hell just for thinking about it, and she'd had a torrid time of it growing up. She told me that her father had once brought in a sort of 'sexual exorcist' to 'purify' her when he discovered the content of some of her sexual fantasies in a teenage diary.

'I was – I am – a complete mess,' she told me sincerely. 'I had to run away. I had to escape.' So, here she was, with the rest of us.

Celeste was from northern France. She was tall, with long dark hair and a round face. She wore dark-rimmed spectacles that made her look like a librarian. She told me that she'd had a nervous breakdown over things she would rather not talk about, and now suffered from depression and anxiety. As we sat in a coffee shop in the centre of Moscow, I remember thinking how hard she must have found this experience. It had quickly become apparent that, living conditions aside, it wasn't going to be a walk in the park.

We were contracted to work long hours and our English classes were spread out across various locations, all over the city. We could have a class of rebellious teenagers – who didn't really want to be there, but whose parents believed it was imperative for their future careers that they learned English from a native speaker – at Elektrozavodskaya, in the north-west of the city, followed by a class of rowdy ten-year-olds near Sportivnaya, on the other side of Moscow. We would race around on the beautiful, crowded Metro system, cramming into carriages like tinned sardines as the doors closed behind us, starting work at 7.30 a.m. each day and sometimes not finishing our final class until 9 p.m. If you factored in how emotionally demanding full-time teaching can be and the need to prepare classes each evening, we were run off our feet.

Slowly, over time, the relentless and unforgiving nature of the job, the school and life in Moscow began to take its toll. Our soft underbellies were gradually exposed and, in different ways, we began to creak at the seams. Taking a day off for stress or mental well-being was out of the question; if you were sick, then you didn't get paid, and the Russians did not seem to have a great deal of time or empathy where mental health or exhaustion were concerned. Over time, these struggles felt increasingly lonely, and we had no sense that anybody really cared about them or us.

Celeste broke first. I heard rumours that she hadn't shown up to her classes for a few days and the school hadn't been able to contact her. Kathy and I were concerned and went to check up on her. When we entered her apartment, she was already in the process of packing. She had been crying and didn't look well. Her face was red and puffy, and she was slowly and methodically folding up clothes and arranging them in neat, organized piles on the bed, next to a large, open suitcase.

'I'm sick of this fucking shithole,' she said quietly, in her soft French accent. 'This isn't what I needed at all. I came here to try to get better, but it's fucking killing me. Nobody gives a fuck here either.'

We told her that *we* gave a fuck about her, and it had the

desired effect, because a small, politely grateful smile found its way onto her face. We all knew what she meant. And she was right – this wasn't the place you were likely to find what was most needed when you were feeling mentally and emotionally vulnerable. Compassion, warmth, empathic relationships, security, stability, tranquillity and hope were in short supply. Celeste had booked a flight back to Paris the very next day, and we never saw her again.

It was Christmas that really underscored the fact that Celeste's departure was just the tip of the iceberg. The Russians didn't celebrate Christmas on 25 December like we did – it was just another working day for them. We ate a makeshift Christmas dinner and held our own 'celebration' at Kathy's apartment. We shared stories about our families and Christmases back home, and talked about how isolated and disconnected we felt to be so far away from it all. We reminisced about things we missed in our home countries, like English pubs, Walkers crisps and Sunday roasts.

When we were feeling that way en masse, I'm not sure we were always good for each other. Psychologists Gerald Haeffel and Jennifer Hames, of the University of Notre Dame in the US, have provided experimental evidence that depressive thinking can be contagious, and we were living proof of that hypothesis. By Christmas evening, things had taken a turn for the worse. Kathy called us all to the bathroom, where we saw Jon sitting fully clothed in the empty bath. He was disgustingly drunk, had been snorting something through a rolled-up 1,000-rouble note, and was crying while holding a razor blade in his left hand. There was panic and desperation in his voice as the tears fell from his cheeks into the dirty cream tub. He said that he couldn't take it any longer, he didn't want to be here any more and he didn't know what to do. Kirsty and I managed to calm him down by sitting with him for hours and talking it through. We spoke soothingly to him until he finally fell asleep right there in the bath. I carried him to the bedroom and Kirsty sat with him, stroking his head lovingly, like a mother caring for a sick child. He seemed genuinely soothed.

Jon was the next to leave Moscow. Like Celeste, he started missing his classes because he simply didn't have the emotional energy to keep going. I met him for coffee, and he very calmly told me that he'd been sacked that day and would be heading home next week, without pay. There was a sense of relief in his voice, and I think he was genuinely pleased that he'd finally stopped kicking and had given up on whatever it was he was hoping to achieve by being here. He also had a renewed sense of hope because, he informed me, he was in love again. He'd been speaking on the phone with someone called Debs over the last few weeks. She was the ex-girlfriend of one of his old friends, had a two-year-old daughter and was pregnant with another child. Jon told me that they'd fallen in love during these telephone conversations and he had decided to give it a go. He was going to return to England, move in with Debs and help her to raise her children.

'I know it sounds crazy,' he said, 'but I love her, you know?'

He seemed genuinely convinced that his life was going to be OK and that he had found meaning again. We don't speak much now, but he sends me a text every Christmas, and, for some reason, always remembers my birthday without fail.

Shortly after that, Kathy went back to her abusive boyfriend in Massachusetts. They had been speaking more and more during her time in Moscow, and she told me that they missed each other and were 'meant to be together'. She too seemed happy and hopeful on the day she left.

Kirsty met an American wrestler on the internet, who happened to be travelling in Moscow. Apparently, he was exactly what she'd always been looking for in the bedroom and their sexual compatibility became the platform from which their love would flourish. She moved back to America with him.

I felt lonelier than ever when they had gone. In a strange way, they had been my family, for a short while. Like most families – or mine, at least – they were highly dysfunctional and quite draining at times, but nonetheless we had created an unlikely sense of solidarity and camaraderie. I had become used to Moscow's rough edges by now too. I was no longer disturbed by the fact that my apartment block didn't have a door, that the communal parts permanently stank of urine, that gangs of youths got drunk in the hallway, or by the fact that there were no street lights and that people were generally unsympathetic and steely. I could feel myself hardening, adapting and evolving.

One night, as I sat alone in my room, I suddenly realized with striking clarity that I wanted to go home. It dawned on me that it was my time to leave too. I booked a flight and left the following week, without working out my notice.

Zeek's 'two-year party' turned into a fifteen-year party. He still lives in Moscow and somehow found his way into the Russian financial sector through his contacts. In the end, perhaps he was the only one who found a lasting sense of belonging in Moscow. Another way of looking at it is that he was the only one of us who found Moscow's bright lights and crazy party scene sufficient distraction from the loneliness that had always lived inside him.

'Mondays are for Jasmine James'

In an interview published in *Rolling Stone*, David Foster Wallace made a prediction. He argued that technology was going to get better and better. And, because of this, he went on to predict that it would get easier, more convenient and more pleasurable to sit alone with images on a screen that were provided by people who didn't really care for us, but simply wanted our money. 'That's fine in low doses,' he suggested, but, if it's the main component of your diet, 'in a meaningful way, you're gonna die . . .'[8]

In many ways, internet pornography mirrors core elements of consumer culture. It's no different from Amazon or Netflix in the sense that people are seductively drawn into a virtually endless array of choice about *what* to consume, they're given a sense of immediate gratification when – or if – they can decide what to consume, and they are provided with a bespoke product that caters to the consumer's every whim in relation to personal tastes and preferences. And, just like Amazon or Netflix, it's possible to imagine people spending years of their lives simply deciding what to consume.

You might argue there are distinctions to be made, of course, because pornography is about sex and relationships, isn't it? But, then again, is it *really*? It's a technological product and it's designed to tap into your neurological apparatus to the extent that you can manufacture an orgasm. But is it really relational, given that it's devoid of human contact, care for the other, love, compassion and empathy? In his 2007 book of essays *Consider the Lobster*, Foster Wallace argued that the pornography addict, like most addicts, 'desires to be blinded, to live in a dream'. The way he saw it, porn addicts are trying to 'eliminate from their consciousness the world outside pornography, and this includes everything from their family and friends or last Sunday's sermon to the political situation in the Middle East. In engaging in such elimination, the viewer reduces himself. He becomes stupid.'[9]

Mark was a living, breathing corroboration of Foster Wallace's prophecy. I first met him as a student in a psychology class I taught well over a decade ago, and he subsequently volunteered as a participant in a research project exploring male experiences of internet pornography use and intimate relationships.

From the beginning, Mark gave me the impression that life was a bit of an uphill struggle for him. His dark hair was never brushed, and you instinctively knew he wasn't cultivating the 'just-got-out-of-bed' look some of the other students went in for. He always had extremely dark circles around sunken eyes, which were themselves shadowy and permanently filled with a murderous expression. I felt as though he was deeply disturbed. He skulked around with a macabre expression on his face that could be described as vampirical, which made it seem as though he was a constantly tortured soul. He wore the same clothes every time I saw him: a dirty beige anorak that he never took off, even when the temperature was sweltering, causing him to sweat profusely; slightly baggy chinos; and a pair of what my grandma would have described as 'sensible black school shoes'. In the nicest possible way, he looked like a slightly rotund Count Dracula disguised as an ornithologist.

He always sat at the back of the class, alone, avoiding

sitting next to or near other students as far as was possible. He would be glistening with perspiration, scowling, glaring, staring darkly at whoever was speaking. I remember I frequently felt uncomfortable around him simply because of the malevolent expression he wore. I was never quite sure whether I might have inadvertently offended or upset him, but in fact he seemed to be this way with everyone. Of course, I kept all this to myself and treated him with nothing but dignity and respect. Sometimes, people's expressions are not an accurate reflection of what's going on inside – but, with Mark, I came to learn, the darkness ran deep.

Discussing the topic of attachment theory in a series of lectures triggered something for Mark. I've noticed that attachment is often a provocative, sometimes painful topic for students to explore, because it can prompt some people to engage in deeply introspective exploration of previously unexcavated territory in their lives or closest relationships. After a couple of lectures, Mark began to follow me around like a lost puppy. He would hang around after class to talk and follow me back to my office; you didn't need to be a genius to work out that he had things he needed to get off his chest. He would simply sit himself down on one of the blue meeting chairs against the wall of my office and talk for hours.

It started with questions, requests for clarification about the finer points of Bowlby's attachment theory, and various reflections on things we'd discussed in class. But this was his way of testing the waters before we moved on to what he really wanted to talk about. He was particularly eager to sign himself up for a research project I was conducting on internet pornography. At first, I thought this was just his way of seizing an opportunity to be listened to, but he said it was because he felt his experiences were an important part of his story and he wanted to explore it with me in a series of interviews.

Mark told me in our first interview that his parents were 'pathologically permissive'. He said that his mum had severe mental-health problems. 'She would do things like run out of the house at two in the morning, banging on neighbours' doors to verbally abuse them for allegedly rummaging through her rubbish bins as part of some sort of mythical conspiracy against her,' he reflected. 'She's off her rocker.' His dad paid a heavy price for caring for his mum, Mark said, and was now, 'half-crazy himself'.

Mark remembered discovering internet pornography when he was around ten years old.

'Yeah,' he said, staring darkly out of the window, 'I had my own computer in my room and my parents didn't place any restrictions on my internet use whatsoever, so I quickly found porn.' He paused. 'There are so many rabbit holes, and one fetish or subgenre can quickly lead to another, until, before you know it, you're watching simulated rape, violent sex, gang bangs and all sorts of crazy shit.

'I realized my parents were different when they walked in on me one night, when I was about eleven. I was watching a gang bang, or something deeply inappropriate, alone in my room. The light was off and my computer screen lit up the room like a sordid shrine, and they walked in together and clearly saw it. You couldn't miss it. I thought, Oh, fuck. I'm in deep shit now. But they didn't say anything, just sort of smiled and walked out.'

He told me he wished they had punished him that night, or scolded him – smacked him, even – anything to offer some sort of behavioural containment, but they didn't – and Mark fell into an unbridled, unregulated vortex of internet pornography from which he felt he had not yet escaped.

Research commissioned by the British Board of Film Classification has suggested that it is not uncommon for children as young as seven to stumble across pornography on the internet. Around 62 per cent of eleven- to thirteen-year-olds who report that they have been exposed to pornography stumble across it unintentionally.[10]

My first exposure to pornography happened back in 1989, just before the rise of the global internet. I also stumbled upon it unintentionally, but it was different then. My brother and I discovered a pile of what would now be considered soft adult magazines, under an old leather sports bag at the back of Dad's wardrobe, which we didn't usually dare touch because of the spiders living there. Mum hurriedly tidied them away and told us not to go near them again, and they were gone before we'd had a chance to question why anyone would want to keep collections of glossy photographs of semi-naked women.

Mark's introduction to pornography was very different. For about a decade, through his formative years, he'd been given free rein in relation to internet pornography use and his sexual development had clearly been shaped, even warped, by these experiences.

'You wake up in the morning,' he reflected, 'open a page, and it leads to a Pandora's box of other visuals, windows, menus. There have probably been days when I saw two hundred vaginas before I got out of bed.'

He continued, 'There's an endless, limitless mass of different genres, subgenres, categories and sexual fetishes to explore, and some of them are dark, man.' He looked at me with those panicked, sunken eyes, as though he was warning me about a monster that lived in the woods.

*

In the end, a group of emotionally vulnerable young English speakers, typically from North America, Britain, Australia and various other Western European nations, wound up in Moscow, helping private schools make large sums of money by offering expensive English language courses to Russian elites. Native English speakers were all the rage in Moscow at the time, and schools wanted them at the front of the classroom wherever possible. But it was clear from the beginning that our psychological and emotional welfare was much less important to the school than our mother tongue. We were paid badly, worked extremely hard and were undoubtedly exploited.

It was a time in my life when I felt alone in the world; rudderless and without a map. Perhaps Moscow was an attempt to start over, wipe the slate clean, to pitch up in a completely alien place where nobody knew me and try to create a new narrative. It quickly became apparent that I wasn't alone – everyone else felt just the same.

I met Zeek at Sheremetyevo airport on my arrival. He was a happy-go-lucky New Yorker who had been contracted to work at the same school as me. He had a distinctive Roman nose, dark, ruffled hair, and he was wearing a hoody and baggy jeans. He told me how excited he was about all the 'beautiful Russian chicks' and how he was in Moscow for a 'two-year party, dude'.

After we had reclaimed our baggage, we met Lena, a polite but decidedly frosty middle-aged woman who was the representative from the language school charged with locating us at the airport and dropping us to the apartments we'd be living in for the next year or so. Our driver, Igor, was frostier still; a burly middle-aged Russian man, he did not acknowledge us in any way for the entire journey, and the loud, cheesy Russian pop music he played on the radio ensured that we had to shout if we wanted to communicate.

Mark had a girlfriend, Katie, and he seemed to love her very much. They had been together since school, and she had moved in with him when he came to study at the university. His girlfriend knew nothing about his experiences of using internet pornography. It was something he felt deeply ashamed of, and he had not found the courage to talk about it with her for fear of rejection and because of the self-loathing he experienced when he reflected on it. But there was no disputing the fact that it had impacted his relationship.

'In order to come, you know, I've got to resort to playing scenes in my head that I've seen while viewing porn. Something is lost there. I can't be *with* my girlfriend, because I'm inside my own head with a set of distorted ideas about what sex ought to be,' he told me.

He explained how it worked, how he'd come to 'orchestrate' or tailor his experiences of sexual arousal in accordance with the consumer-orientated features of modern-day internet pornography.

'You see, you're constantly synthesizing an orgasm based on dozens of shots or particular parts of particular videos,' he began. 'You're looking for the one small stimulus out of the millions that are available that will be the one you "finish" to, and you still don't finish . . . How does that not affect the psychology of having a relationship with somebody?' he asked me incredulously.

Harvard psychology professor, Deirdre Barrett, has suggested that internet pornography is what she has termed a 'supernormal stimulus'.[11] It's essentially an artificial exaggeration of the environmental factors from which we have naturally evolved to become sexually aroused. As Barrett points out, it has been demonstrated that instinctive behaviours across a range of species can be 'hijacked' when we create 'supernormal versions' of normal stimuli. For example, suppose a female bird's instinct is to nurture her small, speckled eggs. She will abandon them when presented with the option of nurturing larger, more heavily patterned artificial 'exaggerations' of those very same eggs. Over time, with repeated exposure to the artificially exaggerated eggs, she will lose interest completely in the normal eggs, as though her instinct towards them has been overridden or hijacked by the supernormal eggs. The normal eggs simply don't cut it any longer.

In a similar way, internet pornography has been thought of as a supernormal sexual experience. People become aroused by watching supernormal bodies having supernormal sex, they become accustomed to selecting these supernormal virtual experiences from seemingly infinite options, and have the possibility to refine, replay, pause and rewind at will. In short, for the internet-porn user, an orgasm can be as bespoke as their morning coffee.

Physiologist Gary Wilson has been a pioneer in relation to the neuroscience of porn, and he argues that people's responses to real sex can be dampened by overexposure to supernormal sex. In his TED talk, 'The Great Porn Experiment', Wilson discusses the evidence in support of terms such as 'porn-induced erectile dysfunction', highlighting issues in heavy users, such as numbed pleasure responses for normal sexual experiences and addictive craving for hits of more supernormal pornographic material.[12]

'Mondays are for Jasmine James, Tuesdays for Sasha Grey. I always look forward to Thursdays the most – Jenna Jameson,' Mark told me in an interview. 'Then, on the weekends, I'm hanging out with my girlfriend. I don't like to believe that porn is invading what I have with my girlfriend. I want to sexually connect with her. I really had to bite my lip when she asked me recently why she's always the one to initiate things.' He paused. 'She seemed hurt and confused. But she was right, you know. I guess I'm removed from her sexually and intimately. It's like all that time with porn is subduing any physical desire for my girlfriend. And, in some weird way, my emotional need for her too.'

David Foster Wallace describes the act of watching pornography as 'a fantasy relationship with somebody who is not real, strictly to stimulate a neurological response' of 'pure, unalloyed pleasure'.[13] Mark was like a human lab rat whose adolescent life had unwittingly verified Foster Wallace's hypothesis. He was caught in a web, trapped with neurological apparatus that had been shaped around a warped, supernormal idea of what sex *is*.

One moody afternoon in my office, the tears started falling from Mark's dark eyes and he placed his head in his hands, tightly grabbing handfuls of his scruffy hair. He spoke as though he simply didn't know how to escape.

'I don't want to lose her,' he told me. 'I love her and she's so important to me. She's my chance to have a different life, a life that's nothing like the one my parents had or the one I have now. But I don't know how to change who I've become – in a sexual sense. Do you realize, I've fantasized so many times about raping my girlfriend, with other guys, in a sort of replication of the hundreds of porn scenes I've seen? What sort of monster does that make me?' he despaired. 'I can't connect to her sexually without sort of "plugging her into" porn. I feel guilty every time I see her. I don't want her to know that this is who I am.'

There was a shade of loneliness inside Mark that I will never forget. He had fallen into an abyss, a world of immediate sexual pleasure, instant gratification, supernormal stimuli and exaggerated, unreal sexual experiences. The seductive abyss had warped and distorted his sexual identity and functioning, to the extent that intimacy in the real world now felt alien and out of reach. He was ashamed of this truth – that he couldn't connect with his girlfriend because that's not what sex meant to him any longer and 'normal sex' just didn't arouse him. In Mark's case, Foster Wallace was right. It is easy to fall into a convenient world where we sit alone with images on a screen that offer us unlimited, unbridled, exaggerated pleasure, but, if that's the staple of your diet, in a meaningful way, something is going to die – and something *had* died inside Mark.

There is a growing body of literature in sex and relationship therapy that points to an emergent epidemic of loneliness and an absence of intimacy in human relationships that is explicitly connected to how internet pornography transforms our experience and understanding of sex. American family researchers, Spencer Zitzman and Mark Butler, have explored how partners of heavy porn users experience their intimate relationships. They describe a lonely, disconnected terrain, where people are increasingly aware that their partners see them through a pornographic filter. One woman, Ann, told them, 'I felt used in our marriage, like I was just there for his gratification.' Another, Mary, reported, 'It took a long time for me to feel like I could even have sex with him again because I always felt like he was viewing somebody else. Even when another person doesn't really exist it still feels like someone else has been brought into our relationship. In some ways, it's like he's had a million affairs.'[14]

Towards the end of our interviews, Mark told me that he'd decided to seek professional help and support for what he was going through, and that he'd been referred by his GP to a psychiatrist. He simply did not know how to unravel the tangled mess in which he found himself and he knew it was taking a toll on his mental health. During our time together, I learned from Mark that there's a sense of emptiness that drives us towards the seductive pleasures that porn and other addictive consumer technologies promise. As a lonely, lost child, he simply wandered into the forest, like Hansel and Gretel, and was drawn to the enticing temptations he encountered there. Once inside, he was trapped, in a kind of toxic vortex that disconnected him from the world.

Google something like 'how to beat loneliness' and your search result will be endless articles entitled 'Twelve ways to beat loneliness', 'Eighteen ways to overcome loneliness', 'Fifteen things to do if you're feeling lonely', or 'Loneliness is a trap: find out how to break free'. The first thing you learn is that it's now fashionable in pop media to pick a number, as low as five or perhaps as high as twenty-seven, and then compile a list of ways to distract people from, or alleviate, their feelings of loneliness. The second thing is that loneliness is commonly seen as a trap to be escaped.

Loneliness was a dirty word for many people I talked to. 'I'm not one of those sad "lonely people", you know, young man!' Margaret, who was seventy-six years old, told me as I arrived one day for an interview. This was a common obstacle I encountered at the beginning of many conversations. People didn't like admitting to feelings of loneliness, even though they are remarkably common. They seemed to feel that identifying as lonely was a sign that something was wrong with them. Our experiences during the Loneliness Project taught us that, ostensibly, loneliness is thought of as a pathology. The consequence of this is a stigma we needed to get past before we could explore and understand people's feelings of loneliness.

The social psychiatrist, Debasish Basu, has suggested that, if loneliness is thought of as a disease, then we can expect medicine to look for its biological, neurological and pharmacological cause and origin.[15] If it is conceptualized as a pathology, then we can expect medicine to *try* to identify its outcome, prognosis and treatment. We noticed that people's idea of loneliness as some sort of defect made them reluctant to admit to it, share it or associate with it. They wanted to get as far away as possible from loneliness, to avoid or escape it, and saw it as an unpalatable label slapped on their forehead.

A concern about medicalizing loneliness is that it could be an inescapable part of being human. If you look hard enough, loneliness is everywhere: under the sofa, behind the door, at the back of the closet. In various guises, in different shades, in countless ways, loneliness is all around us, even if we don't care to admit it. To pathologize it, in all of its images, risks pathologizing part of the human condition. Perhaps the most brutal manifestations of loneliness are worthy of medical attention. But I wonder whether these more explicit presentations of loneliness have somehow hijacked the meaning of subtler experiences of loneliness that are part of most people's existence. The medicalization of loneliness increases the risk of its stigmatization.

Research by Dr Manuela Barreto and her colleagues has suggested that there is already a powerful stigma attached to loneliness.[16] And this stigma pervades individualist and collectivist societies, men and women alike, the young and the old. Loneliness is already something we collectively see as 'toxic'. It's understandable, then, that we might seek to divert our attention away from loneliness with endless and immediate gratifications, or with the help of Google-generated quick fixes.

In his novel, *The Pale King*, David Foster Wallace makes the astute point that perhaps the essence of our discomfort with things like dullness or boredom is that these psychic states fail 'to provide enough stimulation to distract people from some other, deeper type of pain that is always there, if only in an ambient low-level way, and which most of us spend nearly all our time and energy trying to distract ourselves from'.[17] People can try to escape *feelings* of loneliness and emptiness because they are afraid of them. I feel as though that's at least part of the story of how Mark ended up in the challenging predicament in which he found himself.

PART FOUR

OUTSIDERS

The *Shidu*

It's 1998. I'm an A-level student at sixth-form college in Cambridge. I spend my time struggling to apply myself to my studies, hanging out with my girlfriend, playing football and smoking Lambert & Butler Original Silvers behind the bike sheds because I perceive that it will help me fit in with my new friends.

While I'm wrestling with the tail end of my adolescence, a small boy in a town called Quanjiao, in the Anhui province of central China, is sleeping. He was born during the one-child policy period, implemented by the Chinese government between 1980 and 2015, and lives with his mother and father, and his grandma. His grandma is his rock. She has cared for him through thick and thin, including during those long months when his mother got sick and stayed in the hospital, and it was not clear whether or not she would survive.

He has started waking up during the night. He wakes up terrified, floored by the realization that one day he is going to die and so are all of the people he loves – his grandma, his mother and his father. He cries because it frightens him. His mother tries to comfort him, tells him not to worry, not to be silly. Most children eventually comprehend death as an inevitable and irreversible cessation of bodily function that happens to all living things. Like most children, he has reached an existential milestone – the realization that he is finite.

For the small boy, this will turn out to be more than the

typical face-to-face encounter with a brutal existential reality. It will also mark a calling from within, the beginning of a quest for understanding, and a life pathway. He doesn't know it yet, but a love for Japanese anime will kindle his interest in the Japanese language and culture. He will go on to learn Japanese. He will move to Japan to study religion, where his preoccupation and thirst for knowledge about death and dying will reignite. Fate will lead him approximately 5,632 miles away from home, to the UK, where he will dedicate himself to the study of loss and bereavement.

It's 2018. Our paths cross in a tired classroom in the 3-East building of the Claverton Down campus at the University of Bath. Catering have delivered the standard-issue selection of sandwiches, crinkle-cut crisps, bottles of orange juice, a selection of fruit, and caddies of tea and coffee. I am an examiner for his doctoral thesis, a fascinating series of interviews with *Shidu* parents in China. In an article that he will go on to publish in the *Journal of Population Aging* in 2022, he will note that the term *Shidu* 'refers to a group of Chinese parents who were subject to the One-Child Policy but whose only child has died'.[1] The essence of his doctorate is that the *Shidu* endure particularly distressing experiences of grief and unique challenges to their physical and emotional well-being. In a society where adult children predominantly care for older people, he argues, 'childless *Shidu* parents inevitably face a life of having no primary caregivers as they age'.

I reflect on the unique shade of loneliness revealed in his work. I get glimpses of what it feels like for the *Shidu* in some powerful interviews he has conducted. The interviews help me to realize that this specific population of Chinese people experiences a unique kind of loneliness and existential threat.

Guoping, a man in his sixties who has lost his only son, said, 'I had looked forward to having a grandchild who would call me "Grandad", but now this will never happen.' Xu, also in his sixties, expresses that, 'I feel I am a lonely old man abandoned by society. No one really cares about how much I miss my only son. No one will organize and attend my funeral and visit my grave. My family line is cut off, so I will inevitably be abandoned after I die.' And Hou, a woman in her fifties, said, 'I am really concerned about my future. Who is going to look after me, cook and wash clothes for me? I am not sure how I would take my last breath . . . I may die of starving or thirst. And people would not find my body until it gets rotten and smells.'

The *Shidu* feared that the loss of their only child not only robbed them of access to familial care in old age, but also of the opportunity to be remembered beyond death, to experience the joys of grandparenting and the possibility that their family might carry on, long after they had gone. I am touched by the fact that, thanks to this doctoral thesis and ensuing work, the loneliness of the *Shidu* and their struggles with such unique experiences of death and bereavement have not been forgotten, relegated to the annals of Chinese history. Instead, the *Shidu* have been granted a voice by that small boy from Quanjiao, who followed his intellectual and spiritual curiosity and matured into an adult who cared enough to understand and explore these people's predicament.

Chao is now thirty-four years old. He has short, cropped black hair, and a quiet, unassuming presence that makes you feel at ease when you talk to him. We sat in my office on a rainy November morning, and I interviewed him about the ways in which loneliness has been a part of his life.

'Well, in a sense, I've been losing relationships my entire life, simply because of the nature of my studies, career and how my life has taken shape,' he told me.

He was referring to the fact that his career and studies have meant that he hasn't ever been able to put down permanent roots. His passion and interest in Japanese language and culture led him to a Chinese university not far from the border with Russia, where he studied the Japanese language for four years. From there, he moved to Japan, where he studied religion. And, after five years in Japan, he moved on to the UK, where he studied for a doctorate in bereavement. He is now a reputable scholar in his field, with a postdoctoral position at University College London.

'And, because of that, I think I'm actually quite sensitive when it comes to human relationships,' he reflected. 'I'll give you a small example of how relational insecurity affects me. Every time I go to an academic conference, for example – let's say I make friends there – I always feel, the night before the conference ends and I take to my bed, that there's a sadness inside me. Like, "Great, I've made some connections here, but once the conference has ended it is most likely I'll never see them again." It's happened a lot in my life. I don't like losing things or people. I'm preoccupied with loss.'

I thought about what he was saying. 'I guess it's no surprise that you've ended up as a bereavement researcher then?' I ventured.

He laughed. 'The reason *why* I have embarked on a career studying bereavement is because I have always been afraid of losing people – either losing them to death, or losing them during life.

'Every summer, as a child, back in China, I would wake

up in the night and try to explain to my mum the terror I felt about the fact that I was going to die – and the people I loved were going to die,' he continued. 'I could neither understand it nor accept it. My mum just thought I was silly. You see, in China there's a real culture of "death denial". People try very hard *not* to think about it. I think that's why, when people in China are nearing death, they tend to panic. Because, if you haven't allowed death in, or really contemplated it, then the level of fear can be quite . . . traumatic,' he explained.

'So, in that sense,' I asked him, 'doesn't that make you quite unique in Chinese culture? Because you're someone who genuinely has embraced the idea of death and loss, in the work you do? Your whole career is about *not* denying death, isn't it?'

'Well,' he pondered, 'I'm not denying death in what I do. But that doesn't mean I'm not still really afraid of it. I guess I feel that the best way for me to face that sort of existential fear is to at least *try* to understand it.'

He told me that it has always been important for him to follow his own pathway.

'I think my instinct in wanting to do something unique with my life and follow my pathway led me to feel like I don't want to spend my life in the same way everybody else does in China. I have just followed my instincts,' he reflected. 'The cousins I grew up with, for example, they all have very different lives to me now. They are all married, with children, and have office jobs, which is a classic Chinese lifestyle for someone my age. In Chinese culture, you *can* be unique, but you have to be prepared for people to think you are a bit weird.' He laughed.

Chao talked about the essence of his own loneliness being rooted to what he called 'double isolation'. Academic Jonas Olofsson has researched such experiences in Swedish migrants. In his study, a woman called Silvia, originally from Serbia, summed up the concept succinctly: 'I was seventeen years old when I got to Sweden. But I am still a foreigner both in Sweden and when I go back to Serbia. It feels like living in a permanent limbo.'[2]

Chao described something similar: 'My biography feels like it's only half rooted in China now,' he reflected. 'Remember, I left China when I was maybe nineteen years old, and now I'm, what, thirty-four? That's half of my life spent outside my country. Which is quite interesting.'

He continued, 'I still feel like any "roots" I have *are* in China, because my parents, my extended family are still living there. But I feel an increasing lack of connection with people in China now. I was very close to my cousins, for example, and we grew up together. But we have less and less in common now. They are still living there, but we are not that close any more,' he reflected.

'Whenever I think about my hometown, my memories are what they were when I was a high-school student. So, firstly, whenever I go back there, I physically don't recognize the town any longer. It's not the same place that I left.'

Like much of China, Quanjiao, he told me, has been subject to rapid urban development over the last twenty years.

'Secondly, when I used to go to the supermarket, for example, as a teenager, I knew everyone – friends, neighbours, shopkeepers. Now, if I go back, I am an outsider. It's my hometown, but I don't know anyone, and no one knows me. My only connection with that place now is my family.'

For anyone who moves away from their hometown, it is perhaps not surprising to drift out of touch with the place that once felt so familiar. I recognized the feeling, to a lesser extent, from trips back to Cambridge to visit family after decades of living elsewhere. But the essence of the 'double isolation' to which Chao was referring is in the fact that one's new location is as alienating as the old. He told me a little more about the double isolation he encounters.

'I very much want to consider the UK as my home. I've been here for some years now and it's a place I could call home. But, at the same time, the expiry date on my visa always reminds me – you don't belong here! At least, not until, or unless, I ever manage to get permanent residency,' he explained. 'So, as much as I might *want* to feel a sense of belonging here, I'm going to get kicked out if I can't get my next job.' He laughed.

'That doesn't sound like it would feel very . . . homely?' I suggested.

Chao agreed. 'I think, at the political or societal level, I don't feel a sense of belonging here, because it's made clear to me that I don't have the permanent rights that other citizens have. The way I describe it is that it's a bit like a death sentence – like I have six months to live – and, if I'm lucky, and I find another job, I *might* get granted a stay of execution and a bit more time on death row. That's how it sometimes feels.

'I always tell my friends here that I try not to buy too many things – especially big things, like furniture, or even a bicycle – because I don't know what happens if I can't continue to stay here.

'I'm always worrying about whether I'll manage to secure another job before the current job expires,' he explained. 'So, in order to maximize the chances of that happening, I spend all of my spare time focusing on my career, so that I can strengthen my CV and make myself as employable as possible. That way, when it's time for me to find a new job, I'm more likely to be an attractive candidate and less likely to get kicked out of the UK.'

Chao was saying that it is his labour that buys him the right to a life in the UK. And, because of that fact, he spends so much time polishing, sharpening and refining his professional identity – the currency he needs to find his next job – that there's not much time left to relax into other aspects of his life.

'So, where's the *loneliness* in that?' I asked him.

'Well, I guess I feel isolated by government policy, on one level. But then there's an existential level too,' he replied. 'Because, no matter how many things I buy here, how many friends I make, how much of a home I build, all of those dimensions of my existence can be effectively cancelled out if they decide not to renew my visa. My *life* here can be erased.

'And then, if I were to go back to China, I'd feel disconnected there, too, because of the fact that my life simply isn't there any longer either. I think that's the essence of the double bind in double isolation,' he argued.

The double isolation many migrants feel is compounded by additional factors that Chao is lucky enough to have avoided. Factors such as language barriers, financial insecurity and lack of educational capital can intensify a sense of isolation in destination countries. In Olofsson's research, a participant originally from Eastern Europe, Ania, explained the sense of isolation that language barriers had created for her. 'It is so important to know the language. Otherwise, you feel completely left out of life, like a zombie, you are trapped,' she told the researchers.

It's 2022. And the small boy from Quanjiao is now a man. He has chosen to follow a call that emerged from inside him long ago, to understand the turbulent relationship humans share with death.

'The path I've taken and the rich rewards and satisfaction that it has brought me,' he explained, 'has been made possible by the oceans I've crossed that have allowed me to learn, study and understand it better.'

I think he is right. He is privileged to have been able to follow his calling and engage in work that might one day help to alleviate the anxieties and lack of understanding of death denial that are so deep-rooted in so many cultures.

'In that sense, I don't regret it,' he continued. 'But, at the same time, it's important to recognize that there are things I have lost, things I have given up, things I have sacrificed in order to follow that path – like connections, roots and a real sense of home.

'And, of course, there's one important thing that sets me apart from the *Shidu* in relation to loneliness. And that's the fact that I have chosen my plight. They didn't.'

'How to Murder Someone With a Teaspoon'

As we sat in my garden on a hot summer afternoon, on a blanket we'd carefully positioned on the grass so that it was half in the sun (satisfying her love of the sun) and half in the shade (because I don't much like being in the sun), she continued her story. She was lying on her belly, looking at the buttercups on the lawn, reflecting on the fact that it had not been mowed for a few weeks. A couple of metres away, our cat Percy was cooling himself, burying his furry grey body into a shaded area underneath a bush.

Natalie had torn the memories and experiences of childhood abuse into tiny little pieces, scattered them and prayed that her body would somehow bury them. At least, that was the plan. As a child, she had become trapped, suspended in abject terror, completely unable to scream for help; she was alone with the memories of trauma and abuse. She had tried desperately to push those memories to the bottom of a metaphorical lake and freeze them over with a thick covering of ice that, in the ensuing years, she hoped would hold and keep them at bay.

Her attempts to anaesthetize everything seemed to work for a while, and she told me that for some years she felt as though she was doing really well. Everything was safely at the bottom of the lake, and outsiders might have been forgiven for thinking that the terrible thing that had happened to her wasn't a part of her story at all.

'I was doing extremely well academically. I was really

social, I had good friends, I had a disco for my thirteenth birthday, and we lived in this lovely big house and went on great holidays,' she began. 'But things suddenly started to slip.

'Amazingly,' she continued, 'I didn't remember any of my trauma at that time, but things were starting to show up. Things were creeping out, dark shadows, like sharks under the water. They were getting closer and closer, and just appeared suddenly. I felt like I was starting to go mad. I couldn't keep a hold of myself, and I couldn't stop whatever was coming from coming – and I didn't even know *what* was coming.

'I felt like everything was happening in the dark and I didn't know what it was. I just knew that it was really terrifying, and that I was afraid, and that I was alone. I didn't have the words to understand what was happening to me, or what was emerging from my subconscious, and I didn't have anyone to help me frame it either.'

The psychoanalyst Stephen Grosz quotes Isak Dinesen in his book *The Examined Life*: 'all sorrows can be borne if you put them into a story or tell a story about them. But if we cannot find a way of telling our story, our story tells us – we dream these stories, we develop symptoms, or we find ourselves acting in ways we don't understand.'[3] I felt as though that was what was happening to Natalie: the story she'd ripped into tiny little pieces was starting to 'tell her'; its fragments were starting to surface, and the fact that it *was* a part of her story was becoming impossible to deny.

Fresh lake ice doesn't have so many cracks in it. But, by the time it is a few inches thick, there are cracks all over the place. Apparently, the thermal shock resistance of ice is lower than most other materials, and the fact that there are over a dozen different types of ice crack means that, eventually, it's going to break. Cracks can form for a myriad of reasons, including a temperature increase, a temperature decrease, wave breaks and tectonic pressure. And, once the cracks have formed, the integrity of the ice sheet is irreparably compromised. Over time, that's what happened to the ice sheet on Natalie's lake. What had separated her from the beasts, demons and memories that lurked beneath the surface suddenly seemed to disintegrate. She was confronted by the horrors that had been down there, and the horrors seemed to sense the ice was cracking and gathered momentum. She felt herself hurtling towards a carnival of terror that had been an undeniable part of her childhood and she was confronted by a part her life she had tried to forget.

'I don't really feel like I had any supportive family, at that time,' she recalled. 'I think they just thought I was a really difficult child. I just remember feeling really, really lonely and sinking deeper and deeper into this world that absolutely terrified me. I don't think I thought anyone could help me, which in hindsight makes sense,' she explained, 'because I *didn't* have anyone to help me when the abuse was actually happening, and I think that pattern just repeated itself when the trauma started to resurface.

'It was just all spiralling, I felt awful and I was afraid, and I didn't know what I was afraid of, but I knew that it was the worst thing in the world. It was a slippery slope, and I was sliding down it, quicker and quicker, and I couldn't stop,' she told me. 'And it got to a point where I just knew, categorically, that I didn't want to be here any more. I felt this complete sense of overwhelmed panic at what I had to face, and I didn't want to be here to face it.'

A terrifying part of Natalie's life was not only chasing her, but it was catching up with her. At this point in our conversation, I noticed Percy had joined us from the shade of his bush. He lay down, close to us, as though he was listening to the story, and I placed my hand on his warm, soft underbelly as she continued.

'So, one day, I was in my room. I was about fourteen. I was crying, and it just dawned on me that I didn't want to face this any more. I absolutely, categorically knew that I didn't want to be here, and I wanted to die.'

Calmly, she walked into her granny's bathroom and opened the cabinet door. 'I knew that my granny had some high-dose codeine and paracetamol tablets in there, in a big brown jar. There were eighty tablets,' she told me. 'They were like big horse tranquilizers, and I systematically started taking them, one by one. At first, I was crying, but then I just became calm and serene. I remember that it became harder to swallow them as my body sort of resisted, as though it knew I was trying to destroy it.'

She still finds it difficult to take paracetamol, even when she has a headache; she has to force them down because her body seems to forever remember that day.

She woke up in hospital. 'I remember them trying to work out how many pills I'd taken.'

She paused. Percy and I listened.

'There were some tablets left in the bottle,' she continued, 'but a lot had been taken. I had my stomach pumped. It was horrible. You have this tube down your throat and my whole body just felt like it had been turned inside out. I was afraid, scared I might be told off, and also worried that people might make me start talking about why I'd done it. Then I'd have to face the very things I was trying to escape.

'I remember a doctor in a white coat telling me that I had very nearly died and asking me whether I had wanted to,' she explained. 'I must have told them that I did want to die, and they kept me in the hospital, on the children's ward, probably because of that. I remember the ward being empty. It was as alone and empty as I felt inside.'

I asked her if she remembered when she came home from hospital.

'I didn't,' she replied. 'It was decided that I would be admitted to the psychiatric unit, which was a separate build- ing. It was an odd mix, a sort of clinical and boarding-school environment rolled into one. I was transferred there from the hospital.'

The psychiatric unit to which she was transferred was exclusively for adolescents and felt a bit like a hotel, with a reception, an entrance lobby and a wide set of stairs in the hallway. She remembered that they had tried to make it feel homely, but also that the clinical, sterile elements made it impossible to disguise the fact that it was really an institution.

One of the first people she met in the psychiatric unit was an older boy who she remembered was called Stephen. He had a diagnosis of schizophrenia and occupied one of the other rooms in the unit.

'He was a big guy, a bit older than me, very tall, and kind of bulky,' she explained. 'I remember that he hit on me really early on. And, at that time, one of my ways of validating my sense of self-worth was through the attention of guys.'

She continued, 'On my first day, he taught me how to murder someone with a teaspoon by bending the head of the spoon backwards and forwards until it comes off and you're left with a spike. You can then stab someone in the carotid artery with it, he told me.'

On her first night alone in the unit, she heard a commo- tion. It turned out to be Stephen. He was screaming and shouting violently, and other people were screaming and shouting at him in return – probably the staff, trying to restrain him.

'There was this slamming, crashing, and really scary noises,' she told me. 'And I was there, on my own in this place, and I didn't know what on earth was going on. In the morning, he was gone, and I walked past his room. The door was ajar, and I saw that his wardrobe was smashed, things were broken, strewn all over the floor, and there was blood smeared all over the walls and ceiling.

'It was a weird system,' she remembered. 'They didn't have nurses . . . They were more like orderlies. In truth, it was a bit like *One Flew Over the Cuckoo's Nest*. But the nurses, or orderlies, weren't wearing uniforms; they were wearing normal clothes. It all felt like they were trying to make you feel like it was your home, when it wasn't your home.

'We had a rota on the wall, and we knew who would be on each shift,' she continued. 'We had people that we really liked and people that we really didn't like. And if it was a day where the shifts were covered by people who had no warmth – well, that was a bad day. There were people I was afraid of and people I was less afraid of.'

I asked her if anyone ever told her how long she would be staying in the psychiatric unit, why she was there or how often she might see her family.

'No,' she replied. 'To begin with, my family would come every week, but I think that dropped off quite quickly.'

It sounded like an incredibly lonely time in her life, and I wondered how she would describe the loneliness she experienced.

'Everything about it was lonely,' she explained, seemingly without needing to reflect. 'And I mean that. *Everything*. Nothing had changed in my life, and I was still dealing with this darkness that was coming out of me from the depths; things were emerging from inside me that were truly terrifying.

'And this place – this "unit" – wasn't going to save me from that,' she continued. 'Maybe it was me, maybe I couldn't let them get close enough to help me? We were all in there together, the other inmates and me, but we weren't helping each other. I actually learned a lot of ways to self-harm in there. I learned ways to shut myself off, too. I went in there not wanting to live, but I came out with an eating disorder and arms that were cut to pieces because I'd perfected the art of self-harm.'

I glanced at the scars on her arms as they glistened in the sun. I asked her what she felt she'd needed at that time of her life.

She thought about it for a while. 'I didn't need that clinical environment, that's for sure,' she explained. 'I had a therapist who would take us to all of these beautiful gardens and tell us to do things like go and find a pine cone and then write about how it made us feel or what it represented. But none of it helped.

'My family weren't able to be what I needed them to be either. What did I need? I needed someone who was warm, who shared with me how scared they were, how much they cared, how much they knew that something was going on – someone who could hold my hand and help me to face it. I think you need your hand held just to get to the stage where you're ready to face that. And I didn't have it. I didn't have anything. And that's an incredibly lonely experience.'

The trauma of the abuse, the terror of the demons that slowly resurfaced, emerging from and climbing out of the cracks in the ice like an army of evil little sprites, the suicide attempt and the cold, clinical, absurd psychiatric unit – these

distinct shades of isolation formed a patchwork quilt of loneliness that characterized Natalie's story. I looked at her, lying
in the sun, and I realized that she had been into much
deeper, darker parts of the forest than I had been. Her
brushes with loneliness had been brutal, beyond what most
human beings would consider tolerable. Yet somehow, here
she was, in the relative safety of the garden, as the breeze
continued to rustle through the trees.

Percy seemed to sense that the conversation had reached
a natural conclusion. He lazily got to his feet, stretched and
arched his back, before lethargically plodding back to the
shade of his bush.

Enid Blyton and the Little Girl from the Village

Rani was born in India in 1955. She told me that she did not emigrate to the UK until after she had married, which was 'very late, by Indian standards', at twenty-eight years old. She was a deeply thoughtful, intelligent woman, who now lived alone after the break-up of her marriage over a decade ago. She had a kindly face and I think I warmed to her because she was, in her own words, 'another self-confessed extreme introvert'. I always feel comforted in the company of my fellow introverts. We understand each other.

In our interview, Rani seemed happy to share the story of her life with me. We drank tea in her living room, quietly sitting in tattered armchairs that were positioned next to the bay window, offering us a view of the street outside.

'I had a very happy childhood,' she told me. 'But I was the youngest of seven siblings, and all of them were much older than me. The sister immediately before me was five years older, so the others were a good ten, fifteen, seventeen years older than I.' She paused to take a sip of her tea. 'I remember my father being a very busy man, but always there for us in a very positive way. And my mum had a very domesticated role, running the home with the help of the typical post-colonial Indian-style servants and gardeners and cooks and what have you. Mum's job was to supervise all of them and make sure we were well fed, well clothed and looked after.'

Rani's father worked in the Indian civil service and his job required them to move frequently. She remembered moving as a defining feature of her childhood.

'I only saw my older siblings during the Diwali and summer holidays, because they were all packed off to boarding schools.'

She acknowledged that the frequent moving around did not make for a very settled childhood.

'Now, when I look back on it, I think that's the thing that sticks most in my memory – the fact that we didn't settle in one place for long enough. Because my dad had a job in the civil service, we changed cities and towns almost on a yearly basis. And, although it was a lot of varied experience in different types of schools and different types of "India", it was lonely as well, because I was one of those introverts that didn't settle immediately and didn't make friends immediately, and, by the time I made friends, it was time to move on to the next place. I was lonely because of the moving around and because I was so much younger than my siblings, who were always away at school.'

Residential mobility is a major predictor of loneliness. Moving is stressful and it inevitably disrupts social networks. Ironically, it is at times of increased stress that people are most likely to need the very social networks that have been disrupted by mobility.

'I didn't make friends easily anyway,' Rani reflected, 'but my chances of making them were hindered even more powerfully by the fact that we never stayed long enough for me to nurture and hold on to a friendship. In the end, I think I sort of gave up on friendship as a viable option for filling up any sense of emptiness I might have felt as a child. My lifestyle just didn't permit me to consider friendship as a way to alleviate my loneliness. So, I found other ways to feel less alone, and books were a major part of that,' she continued.

I was interested to learn that the works of Enid Blyton had

been a significant part of Rani's early attempts to fill up her inner world. The stories provided her with a sense of comfort at a time in her life when she often felt alone and isolated. As a child, I too had lost myself in the adventures of the Famous Five and the Secret Seven. I read them compulsively. My grandparents had a mini collection of Enid Blyton books that I regularly returned to. I would escape into an imaginary world where children raided the pantry for picnics – consisting of things like a leg of ham, a loaf of bread, tins of spam and Victoria sponges – and ran off to have adventures and solve mysteries. Rani explained why she felt so drawn to the stories during her childhood.

'I would sit and read all of my Enid Blyton books. I was a voracious reader!' She laughed. 'All of Enid Blyton's imagination was about Cornish coasts and little white children that had such adventurous times. It was so completely unlike my really tame, lonesome childhood in India. I felt like the characters were my imaginary friends – Julian, Dick, George, Anne and Timmy the dog – they really filled up the emptiness that characterized my life at that time.

'I'll tell you something else that you don't hear every day,' she continued. 'My mother tried to help me feel less alone by literally brokering a deal with a local family to bring me a little companion of my own age.'

She explained to me how her mother had brought her a companion to prevent her feeling lonely – a little girl, who left her own family of nine sisters and came to live in the household.

'She brought a little girl from the village for me because all my siblings were so far away, and she was the same age as I was,' she told me. 'She came to us when we were both eight years old. And then she followed us wherever we went, whichever city we went to, and became a part of our family.'

Rani stared out of the window as she remembered the little girl.

'Mum used to treat her as a servant, this little girl,' she continued, 'and I used to have a lot of conflict about this with Mum, because the way she thought and the way I thought were *very* different. So, anyway, this little girl, Hansa – whose name means "swan" – and I were the best of friends.' She laughed. 'I was determined to welcome her into the little world of stories and imagination that I'd created for myself. She couldn't read, and every story from the Famous Five and the Secret Seven was relayed to her in the greatest of detail! I guess I shared the inner imaginary world I had created for myself with Hansa.'

Hansa went on to marry in her early twenties, and she became a successful businesswoman, with a factory in Delhi importing and exporting clothing.

'She must have been liberated in some way,' Rani reflected, 'because how does an uneducated village girl go on to become a factory owner in India?' She smiled. 'The last time I went to India, a very rich businessman's wife, who had not only married a businessman but had also built up a successful business empire of her own, walked in to give my mum an invitation to her daughter's wedding. And I just sat there, did the whole *namaste* greeting thing, and read my book while Mum talked.

'Then Mum suddenly said, "Rani, do you not know who this is?" And I said, "No." And, lo and behold, it was her, Hansa, the little girl from the village! We both leaped up and ran to each other, hugged and cried.' She laughed again. 'It was just so sweet. I met her again after decades!'

Sometimes, during interviews, I like to ask people if they have any treasured possessions that might help me to appreciate the story they are telling me. The narrative behind our most treasured possessions can be a window to deeper levels of understanding.

'How strange that you should say so!' Rani exclaimed, excitedly. 'Yes, I probably have two or three artefacts in the whole of my house that help me to remember my life in India.'

She eagerly went to retrieve the artefacts and came back with a small brass rabbit and a set of Russian dolls.

'This little brass rabbit was my only toy as a child,' she began. 'Can you imagine, as a two- or three-year-old, having a solitary brass rabbit in the palm of your hand as your only toy?' She laughed. 'That was my only toy! And so, it stands proudly next to my shrine in my bedroom. I don't know what my rabbit is doing there, but it's there.'

Her incomplete set of Russian dolls also meant a lot to her.

'You see, when I was eleven or twelve, we used to live in Calcutta, because my dad was leading the team of engineers that was going to design the first underground railway in Calcutta,' she explained. 'A team of Russian engineers had come to work alongside them, and they left this Russian doll with my dad as a gift, and my dad used to value that doll so much; it had pride of place in the living room, in one of the cabinets.' She paused to reflect. 'And, when I first went back to India from the UK, with my little son, my dad gave that doll to him as a gift. I knew that it meant a lot to him, and he was giving it to my son – so it's always been very special to me.'

When Rani reflected on her adolescence and young adulthood in India, she explained that she felt overprotected – cosseted, even – and would often rebel and push back.

'Oh, I used to have a lot of conflicts with my mum and my dad. I wouldn't be allowed to attend parties. I wouldn't be allowed to go out with my friends after school. My dad would say it's unsafe, and my mum would say, "No, this is not what we Rajput girls do!" and things like that,' she explained.

'Rajput girls', she informed me, was a reference to a large cluster of castes originating from the Indian subcontinent and from which her family descended.

She continued. 'I used to rebel so much. At the age of sixteen, when I went to university, I think one of the ways I rebelled was I began smoking, which is something young women never did in India. And another thing I did was I had a lot of male friends; I always got on much better with men and boys than I did with the women. I used to go about on motorbikes with them, and on scooters. I remember having a really nasty motorbike accident, where the motorbike skidded along the road. But I dared not go home and say, "I've been in a motorbike accident when I went out with this guy!"

'I must have been such a misfit in Indian society,' she reflected. 'I think I've got an awful lot of regrets too. There was a lot of pressure to get married in India, and normally women would get married at say . . . nineteen, twenty or twenty-one. I was twenty-eight when I got married, so I was treated by cousins and all of the family very delicately because they thought I was on the shelf.

'I remember that I was shown an endless, endless line of prospective grooms, and either they didn't like me, or I didn't like them, and nothing came of it,' she told me. 'And I think, in some ways, I felt coerced into getting married – by the overwhelming social pressure in India.

'I think, if I could live my life again, I would say I'd rather be single and independent and wait until I meet somebody that I'd actually *like* to spend my life with. I married someone I didn't want to spend my life with; my marriage was an obligation,' she added. 'Yes, that is one of the big regrets of my life, for sure. There is a loneliness in feeling as though your marriage is little more than an obligation. You never really want to get to know the person because it always feels a little bit like they were forced on you, so you react how people often react to things that are forced on them – you resent those things, push them away, make it your objective not to get to know them. At least, that's how I responded to the whole idea of arranged marriage,' she reflected.

As Rani told me her story, it was clear that she felt that she had been lucky, in the overall scheme of things.

'Of course, as tends to be the case with family, they have posed their challenges, created their fair share of conflict, and at times it felt infuriating,' she told me. 'But, because of the way families operate in India, I have unbelievably close ties with every one of my siblings, and my mum and dad. And, strangely enough, even the cousins that I spent some of my childhood with. Do you know, we don't even have the word "cousins" in Gujarati; we call them *bhai* and *bahan*, which means "sister" and "brother" – and that's exactly what they were to me.' She smiled. 'Yes, I came from a really close-knit family, and that was really huge for me – family bond and family relationships.'

Then, when she came to England, her own children over-took everything and became of paramount importance to her. She told me that, for her, 'the meaning of life and what makes it worth living is intimately connected to relationships.'

She smiled. 'It's relationships that make life worth living, isn't it? And I think, if you measure success that way, I will say I've had an immensely successful life. I've had the most amazing relationships at every stage in my life. Throughout my journey, I've met some amazing people, and it sometimes makes me think, Oh God, life is such a wonderful, unpredictable, rollercoaster of a journey.'

Rani was not aching with loneliness or suffering in the way that others I had spoken to often were. Her life had not been devoid of closeness, intimacy, warmth or security, and she taught me that loneliness isn't always a brutal tyrant. It can come and go. Sometimes it's a quieter presence, like someone humming dulcet tones in the background, or it can be an itch that you're aware you need to scratch, but it isn't all that urgent to attend to.

Towards the end of our interview, Rani began to connect with some of the ways loneliness had permeated her life. Loneliness had undoubtedly visited her during her childhood. In many ways, she had felt like an outsider in Indian society and in the eyes of her family. And she'd lived through a lonely married life in a foreign country. Suddenly, she looked at me with tears in her eyes.

'You know what?' she began. 'I feel the sort of loneliness that only an immigrant really understands. Of course, I have been lucky to find close, beautiful, warm relationships in my life, and they are in my memory, where nobody can take them away. In that sense, the Indian part of me can never die. But, oh, you make me want to cry when I think about the *essence* of my loneliness,' she told me, as the tears started to roll down her cheeks.

'I think you never, ever talk about these things and they go unsaid, unacknowledged, but they are there in the recesses of your mind. I think it's helping me to realize all the really precious things I left behind to come here, in search of God alone knows what, that I never really found.

'I think, as an immigrant, you always feel like a part of your identity is missing, and that becomes more and more profound, and more and more painful towards the end of your life, especially when you realize that the Indian part of your identity might never be a part of you again in the same way it once was.'

*

Later that evening, I sat alone in the kitchen and remembered a paper I'd read by Jonas Olofsson and his colleagues at the University of Malmö in Sweden. Published in a journal called *Nursing Ethics*, it addressed the unique experience of loneliness that older migrants report. An interview with a man the researchers called Fritz – a ninety-two-year-old migrant from Serbia – came to mind. Fritz was approaching the end of his life and he had all but given up. 'I have no wish to live any more,' he told the researchers. 'I pray every night. Dear God. Let me fall asleep and not wake up any more. I do not want to wake up. I mean it. I do not want to fight any more. I am done. I do not hear; I am nearly blind; I can no longer walk. Why the hell should I fight? I have fought. I have fought for life.'

He continued, 'I have been crying for many nights. I cry because I know I will never see my country of origin again. And that hurts so, so much. I can no longer visit my mother's grave, and I feel, so profoundly, that I need "home" before I am done.'[4]

The researchers argued that migration is a lifelong process and the sense of loss in relation to home and cultural identity is not something people just forget. It struck me how important it seemed to be for Fritz, in the final stages of his life, to feel some sense of connection with the place he felt had always been 'home', and how the absence of that connection made the end of his life a lonelier experience. I wondered if, despite Rani's closeness to her family, or perhaps because of it, her yearning for home would intensify as she moved closer to the completion of her life.

Lost, Despite the Map

I didn't ask or expect to be a single parent. I'm not sure anyone who doesn't start out as a single parent ever really expects to become one. It's difficult to say exactly when I became one. Technically, it was the day she left. Perhaps I was, in a sense, already single parenting while we were still together, when it became clear that she probably wasn't going to be able to devote herself to parenting in the ways some parents devote themselves. For reasons that are complex, and of which perhaps not even she is fully aware, she wasn't able to 'choose' parenting.

In the novel *A Little Life*, Hanya Yanagihara writes that parents' worlds are orchestrated by children, 'little despots whose needs . . . dictate every decision, and will for the next ten, fifteen, eighteen years'. She goes on to argue that children provide some people's adulthood with a non-negotiable purpose and direction. They determine what we do with large chunks of our time, how we spend our money and where we go on holiday. Ultimately, 'they give shape to a day, a week, a year, a life'. Children, she concludes, 'are a kind of cartography, and all one has to do is obey the map they present to you on the day they are born'.[5]

I'm not obtuse enough to think everybody can or will accept the map they are handed when a child is born. Some people have other maps that, for whatever reason, they deem more important or are compelled by even stronger forces to follow. I'm also not imperceptive enough to think that all parents who try to accept the map can fully accept it or are invested in obeying it. After all, my mum was effectively a single parent because Dad simply couldn't follow the map – despite the fact that he lived with us for the duration of my childhood. For many, obeying the map feels like a trap, an obligation, an inconvenience, or something too terrifying for them to be able to accept.

The night before she left, I remember how we sat in the living room to talk about what would happen after the separation. I couldn't eat much that evening; my stomach was in knots. My biggest fear was that she would take him away from me, that I'd be relegated to the margins of his life, wouldn't get to see him every day, kiss him goodnight and just have him around. I was terrified that I'd be forced into a position where I'd become one of those single fathers who has no opportunity to be anything other than a mildly interested uncle who buys their child candyfloss at the weekends, gives them twenty-pound notes for their birthday and takes them to McDonald's for a meal that's slightly awkward because parent and child don't really know each other. I thought she was going to take away my opportunity to accept the map. And, that night in the living room, after she'd packed her bags, I braced myself for a battle – a battle in which I wasn't going to simply roll over and concede. A battle in which, if I had revealed my hand, I would have considered fifty-fifty custody a major win. We sat in the living room like two high rollers playing for seriously high stakes.

In the end, it didn't happen that way at all. Instead of tussling over the map, she simply handed it to me, rolled over, no questions asked. In that moment, it was clear that she simply couldn't accept the pathway that had been laid out for her and that we weren't playing for the same stakes. She left the next day and, although she would never be completely absent in his life, she would never again occupy more than a peripheral role in the highs and lows of day-to-day parenting.

I wanted the map. But it is a lonely experience when it is handed to you, and you realize that it is now solely your responsibility to follow it. From now on, I would be single-handedly navigating the challenges and pitfalls of parenting. I didn't have family close by and my social networks were thin on the ground, to say the least. And I wasn't just a single parent, I was a single father, and the data doesn't paint a particularly rosy picture for single fathers.

Families headed by single fathers are a growing demographic, particularly in parts of the world where divorce, separation and non-marital childbearing are increasing. Recent research in *The Lancet*, by Dr Maria Chiu and her colleagues at the University of Toronto, has suggested that there are around three million single-parent families in the UK and 10 per cent of them are single fathers. Interestingly, Chiu's research suggests that single fathers have a much greater risk of premature mortality compared to single mothers and partnered fathers.[6] This seems to be connected to increased prevalence of a variety of risk factors for single fathers, such as poor diet, increased lifestyle stressors, a higher prevalence of chronic health conditions and less than adequate social support. The research also suggests that single fathers are significantly less likely to have meaningful social connections, relationships and networks that they can mobilize to enhance well-being and a sense of belonging. It is particularly hard for single fathers to find people they can confide in, identify with and rely upon.

I was acutely aware that I didn't know anyone who shared my predicament. My male friends or colleagues were all either partnered fathers or child-free. I remember how I used to hope that I might stumble upon a single father, like me, simply so that I didn't feel so different. When Alex started school, I felt as though our family structure stood out. Within the small, close-knit community of overwhelmingly white, middle-class families whose children attended the picture-postcard primary school on the leafy outskirts of Bath, I quickly realized that single fathers were not a thing.

In the school community, most parents were couples who had started families in their mid-thirties, when their careers were established and it was a financially sensible decision. They were high earners, who drove expensive people carriers, lived in idyllic houses and, for the most part, had stereotypically intact family structures, such as you might see happily strolling along a beach on the front cover of a travel brochure. They planned sensible age gaps between siblings and went skiing during the Christmas break. They reflected a neat, tidy, orderly conceptualization of family. Or, at least, that was the impression they gave. They brought in trays of perfectly baked fairy cakes when it was their child's birthday, and baked them as a family on Sunday afternoon during 'family time'.

Of course, they were not unwelcoming, unkind, exclusionary or impolite. And, in many ways, we were part of the same privileged ethnic, socioeconomic, professional and cultural demographic. But I couldn't ignore the fact that Alex and I differed in relation to one thing – our family structure – and, in a close-knit community, that's not a difference that goes unnoticed. For the first time in my relatively privileged life, I felt different, inadequate, incomplete and a bit of an outsider. It wasn't their fault, but I think I resented them because we were not like them. I felt powerless to compensate for what we were missing because I couldn't be a mother *and* a father.

I remember my first awkward, feeble attempt to join in with the school coffee morning, during Alex's first few weeks in reception class. As I walked in, people were polite and welcoming, but it was immediately apparent to me that I was the only dad present. Some mums were busily making the coffee and tea, others kept an eye on and tried to round up the various toddlers that were running around loose like escaped chickens. I eventually took my place on one of the chairs that were positioned in a neat circle so that the mums could watch the younger children play with a box of toys that had been strategically placed in the middle. We sat drinking coffee, watching the toddlers play, as though we were observing an obscure performance. I felt different simply because I didn't have a toddler to watch out for – and because they were all mothers, with what I assumed to be intact family units, their husbands out at work. They had different lives. And, as they talked about their lives with each other, I felt as though they didn't understand mine, and I didn't understand theirs. I sat on my chair, sipping my coffee and politely eating the jammy dodger I'd selected from the Waitrose selection box that was passed around, and I felt decidedly out of place.

In the early days of single parenthood, I felt myself adrift in a turbulent sea. I had to learn to juggle the practicalities of work, school runs, cooking, cleaning, playing, bedtime routines, packed lunches, chickenpox, shopping and everything else that comes with parenting. I was particularly struck by the surprisingly busy social calendars of four-year-olds. There are parties, play dates, sleepovers and activities like 'rugby tots' to navigate. At one stage, it seemed as though we were attending birthday parties almost every week. I spent endless hours watching sweaty, excited little children running around in brightly coloured warehouses with names like Zany Zone or Wacky Warehouse, filled with networks of tunnels, slides, ropes, ladders, mazes and pools of multicoloured plastic balls. Invariably, as the crazy, sugar-fuelled children race around in these warren-like structures, capitalizing on an opportunity to truly let themselves go, some will collide and bump heads as they race blindly through a tunnel, seemingly just running as fast as they can. There are blood-curdling screams from somewhere deep inside the labyrinth, screams which one parent or another instinctively recognizes, in the way that ewes recognize their lamb's cry in a field full of other lambs that all look and sound the same to humans, and a rescue mission is initiated.

At some point, a group of mums rounds up the crazy children because it's time for cake. They eat party food, are given a little bag filled with sweets, plastic toys and something like a tube of bubble mix, and everyone goes home feeling sick, content, accepted and a little bit confused about what it was all about.

I had to try to squeeze my own social life and interests into the recesses of time Alex spent with his mum, or simply learn to fit them around the seemingly endless duties parenting creates. In the beginning, I was trying to do that alongside an overwhelming sense that something was broken in my life that I desperately needed to fix. I felt an urgent need to 'fix' our family structure, and I was acutely aware that I didn't have an intimate connection with another adult.

In the early days, I felt a sense of abandonment and panic,

as though I needed to rectify the situation as quickly as possible. That's what initially led me to the world of dating sites for single parents. It's not really a surprise that entrepreneurial people have capitalized on the market potential in something like 'helping single parents find love again'. Their slogans revolve around ideas like the fact that dating other single parents means you will meet people who automatically 'get you' and contain a key ingredient for your 'perfect match'. I found myself on a date with Anne, a single parent who was training to be a nurse. We met in the city one evening and had dinner in a restaurant before moving on to a cocktail bar she knew. She was attractive, fun and good company, and I noted that she was also incredibly generous, paying for a succession of extremely overpriced cocktails. She kissed me from across the table, a bit out of the blue, boldly leaning over and pulling me towards her. We kissed for a while, and she invited me back to her flat.

In the taxi, she told me that Anne wasn't actually her real name – it was Nandita. She explained that she had used Anne as a cover because she didn't think people would 'respond well' to Nandita. I didn't understand her logic at first, but she told me that the racial connotations of using her real name had resulted in a narrower pool of interest, or attracted the wrong sort of interest, and made it more difficult for her to move forward with finding a new partner. The barriers to developing human connections can be particularly complex for some people.

When we arrived at her apartment, she didn't waste a moment before continuing the kissing we had started back at the bar. She suddenly stopped and walked into the bedroom, gesturing for me to follow. As I followed Anne – or Nandita – to the bedroom, I walked past the open door of the bathroom and got a brief snapshot of how a complete stranger goes about living their day-to-day life. I noticed her clothes spread over the bathroom floor, an orange towel draped over the side of the bath, a pink dressing gown, her toothbrush discarded in the sink. The toothpaste didn't have a lid on it, and the ledge around the bath was filled with half-empty bottles of shampoo, shower gel and other bathroom products. For reasons I do not fully understand, I suddenly felt afraid, as if the ocean in which I had been drowning had washed me up on the shores of somebody else's unfamiliar life, even further away from 'home'. I felt like an alien, and a shiver of fear ran through me as the realization that I didn't want to be there suddenly flooded my body and mind.

I know it's a cliché, but it wasn't her, it was me. I think that a wiser, more knowing part of me realized acutely that sex with a stranger wasn't going to save me in the way I was looking to be saved. A part of me was desperate to cling to an island, any island, to save myself from the lonely ocean in which I found myself. But I think I knew, somewhere inside, that there was no magical paradise here. As the psychoanalyst James Hollis suggested, in the end, 'no one can give me what I most want or need. Only I can.'[7] And the belief that union with another person will somehow 'complete us' or 'make us whole again' is always a projection, a fantasy, an illusion.

In the bedroom, Nandita was waiting for me, fully undressed on the bed. She beckoned me towards her, and I felt the sense of threat, discomfort and unfamiliarity that had materialized inside me as I walked past the bathroom continue to build. When I told her that I thought we really ought to use protection, she suddenly became angry. She made a loud growling noise that I took to reflect a sense of frustration, and she walked over to a chest of drawers in her bedroom that I recognized as being the same one from IKEA that I used to have. She rummaged around for a while in the top draw before returning to the bed and crossly slamming a shiny blue condom wrapper down onto the mattress beside me.

It dawned on me in that moment that this was the very opposite of what I needed. For me, this sort of sexual union with a stranger, in unfamiliar territory, somehow made me feel lonelier. I awkwardly explained to her that I didn't feel comfortable. She wanted me to stay, nonetheless. She said that perhaps I'd feel more comfortable if we slowed things down and just talked for a while. I agreed to lie beside her, and she eventually fell asleep. I lay next to her for a while, looking at the light from the street creeping in through the small gap in the curtains, as her heavy breathing transitioned into weak snoring. The sense of unfamiliarity and discomfort did not dissipate, but further intensified. As I lay in the dark, in an unfamiliar bed, staring at the ceiling, next to a sleeping stranger, I felt more alone than ever.

By three in the morning, I don't think I had slept a wink. I'm not sure why I stayed that long. Obligation? Fear? Paralysis? I quietly got up and let myself out. I walked alone through the city to the train station, hoping to catch the first train home. As I walked through the sleepy streets, under the night sky, I realized that the answer to the acute sense of loneliness I had felt since Alex's mum had left would not be soothed by the sort of 'quick fix' I had been searching for that evening. Panic and feelings of abandonment rarely prove themselves to be astute judges of our best interests, and these sorts of encounters often serve only to exacerbate feelings of loneliness and isolation.

'She's a Lovely Girl, Lady, Old Lady . . . ?'

Ray was seventy-eight years old. He had been a chemistry teacher for most of his working life, moving into the senior management side of the school towards the end of his career. He spoke with a thick northern accent.

'I still miss it to this day,' he told me, as he settled into his leather armchair, folded up his spectacles and placed them on a small, round, mahogany coffee table positioned next to his chair, on which I could see a copy of *The Guardian* newspaper, a pen, the TV remote and a pile of what looked like a combination of bills and junk mail.

'I just enjoyed the challenge each day, and that, to me, was what I loved. Finding new things for pupils to do and learn – I found it really enjoyable,' he reflected. 'I'm full of stories, me. That's how I used to teach. In my sixth form, on a Friday afternoon, the sixth session of the week, I used to say, "Shall we do, say, Krebs cycle or something or other, or shall I just tell you a story?"' He smiled and took a sip of his coffee. 'You can guess what they replied!'

From the very beginning, Ray's wife, Pam, was a focal point in our conversation. He seemed to want to talk about her, and whenever I gently tried to move the conversation on to a slightly different topic, we'd inevitably come back to Pam.

'My wife was a reception teacher for most of her working life too,' he told me. 'She left teaching to have the children, of course, and then, when they were at school, she went back to the profession. So, education is an important part of who we both are.

'We've been married over fifty years, you know – well, fifty-four, to be exact – but Pam has dementia now. That's why we moved here,' he said, gesturing with his arms to help me understand that, by 'here', he meant the gated, well-manicured retirement village around us.

Their home was welcoming, and the sun shone power-fully through the generous patio doors of the living room. Shafts of sunlight illuminated thousands of tiny particles of dust that filled the air, floating around like tiny little insects. I remembered how tranquil it made me feel to watch the random movement patterns of such processions of little dust particles as a child, when I sat in my grandparents' living room on sunny mornings while they drank tea, and I would have a glass of orange squash and a biscuit.

'But she's going downhill more rapidly, these days,' Ray continued. 'Pam's illness developed over the last two and a half years. That was when we made the decision to move here,' he told me. 'We didn't intend to move from where we were, but her illness developed so much that she wasn't allowed to drive. Walking into the village itself became awful for her, because of the traffic and what have you – it was too dangerous for her – so we thought this would be the sensible place.'

Ray had made it clear from the outset that he was against the idea of us talking with or meeting Pam. He felt that she wasn't 'up to it' and that talking to a stranger would 'probably upset her'. So, as was frequently the case when we talked to someone caring for a spouse or partner living with dementia, we didn't get to meet Pam. Careful arrangements had been made to ensure she was not around. She was being looked after by their son, Andy, that day, Ray informed me.

During the ethical approval phase of the Loneliness Project, the issue of dementia and informed consent had arisen. Technically, a diagnosis of dementia does not mean that a person is unable to consent to something. However, it is important that people living with dementia can make a competent judgement. This is usually connected to things like their ability to receive, understand and process information, to appreciate a situation and its consequences, and to weigh up benefits, risks and alternatives. If an individual is deemed unable to give competent consent based upon these factors, then the alternatives are proxy consent – from a family member – or double consent – from the person themselves *and* a family member. The complexities and potential pitfalls that ethical committees reasonably felt this could create for our project meant that we did not have ethical permission to interview people with dementia. The upshot of this was that people with dementia were frequently talked about, but it was as though they were behind a sheet of frosted glass; they were closeted away or taken out for the afternoon, deemed by their spouse or partner too vulnerable or incompetent to engage in the discussion we were having.

Although Pam was notably absent, she was almost all Ray and I talked about.

'We saw the consultant, gosh, the sixteenth of December, I think it was,' he continued. 'It was at the Carlton Centre, in Leeds . . . Pam went in, and I said to her, "Pam, normally, when you see the consultant, he'll say, 'How are you, Pam?' and you'll say, 'I'm fine, I'm fine,'" and I said to her, "This time, please go in and speak the truth."' He paused as he remembered the events. 'So, she went in. "How are you, Pam?" the consultant asked. And Pam said, "Very depressed and very fed up, actually." And, basically, the consultant said, "Well, I can't do anything for you."'

Ray looked at me as though he expected a tut of disapproval, so I obliged and gently shook my head.

'And it is a *fact*, they *can't* do anything for her,' he said, more forcefully. 'So, I said, "Well, what's the point in us coming here, if you can't do anything for her? It's a waste of a journey and it makes her even more depressed." So, we've left it so that Pam doesn't even see the consultant any more.'

He looked out of the window and paused for a short while. I asked if there was any kind of therapeutic or pharmacological support available to her at this stage of her dementia.

'Well,' he said, 'I argue that the medication she's taking isn't doing any good whatsoever. I told the consultant, "It's supposed to be stabilizing the situation, but I don't think it's stabilizing things at all." The consultant said, "Well, if you stop the medication, you might see rapid deterioration." And I said, "Will we?" I'm not so convinced, because there is no medication for what she's got. She's got Lewy body dementia and there's no actual cure. All that she's got is literally the stuff you'd have to take for Alzheimer's, whatever it is, and that's a different condition altogether.'

At this point in the conversation, the essence of Ray and Pam's loneliness was slowly starting to reveal itself.

'This was supposed to be *the* community for us, for her,' he told me, an increasing sense of desperation creeping into his voice. 'The place where she could hold on to the things she loves.'

As he spoke, I began to appreciate just how hard it must be for him to come to terms with the fact that he was slowly losing his wife, watching her become increasingly alienated from the world around them. His words, from this point onwards, were dripping with sadness, anger, frustration and confusion.

'Pam used to belong to a book group – it was such an important part of her life,' he continued. 'Well, at first, she laughed about it, but now she cries at the same time. You know, she taught all those children, over, gosh, goodness knows how many years teaching. Thirty-five years teaching, and she taught all those children to read and write – and now she can't even read herself, and she can't write.'

I noticed a tear rolling down his left cheek.

'It's so cruel to her that she is no longer able to do the things she earned a living doing . . . that she loved doing.'

He stared off into space and I waited for him to gather his composure.

'So, she belonged to a book club,' he continued. 'Well, she's tried the book club here, and she gets so . . . how best to describe it? Frustrated! Because she can't complete a sentence! Frustrated! Because she hasn't been able to read the books. The font size is too small!' he said, incredulously.

'She has to have a relatively large font size to be able to have a chance to read a book now. It has to be a light-ish book, because otherwise it's too heavy for her, and so on and so forth,' he continued. 'There are all these little things that gradually rob her of the things she loves. We've tried audiobooks, but she falls asleep as soon as she starts listening to the thing! I just don't feel they really take it on board in the book group and provide the support I think she needs to hang on to something she loves.'

Ray then said something that really touched me.

'In some ways, I just feel she's a bit like a leper, really, because no one actually wants to get close to her.' He started to cry. 'She's a lovely girl, lady, old lady . . . you know?'

He wept openly.

'I know,' I replied quietly.

The economist, Naila Kabeer, once wrote about a man from Ghana, living with leprosy, who suggested that 'it is neither leprosy nor poverty that kills the leper – but loneliness'.[8] Pam couldn't connect with the world any longer, and it couldn't, or wouldn't, connect with her. Ray was aching for her, for himself, for them both. I sensed his confusion around who Pam was. Was she the 'lovely girl' he fell in love with fifty-four years ago? The 'lovely lady' who had been his loyal and loving companion? Or the 'lovely old lady' who was now burdened with the cruel suffering inflicted by Lewy body dementia?

'I feel very lonely,' he continued. 'Shall I tell you what the real hell of it is? It's just sitting here, like you're already mourning somebody you've lost, yet you're still living with them – it's sad, but it's true.'

He had identified a key feature of spousal loneliness associated with dementia – that the onset of loss and grief begins a long time before death takes hold.

'I've said it to myself many times – "I didn't sign up for this" – I'm being honest. There's a voice in my head, somewhere, that says, "Have I really got ten, fifteen years of this sort of existence left in my life?"' He reflected. 'But you say, "For better or worse," don't you? And I accept that. You don't stand there saying, "If she gets dementia, I don't want to know."'

Ray was nothing if not devoted, but caring for Pam had gradually taken over his existence, to the extent that his life had significantly shrunk. Research into loneliness and dementia has identified this as a common experience for spousal carers.[9]

'I can't leave her behind for anything,' he told me. 'If something happened, if she got up to touch something, had an accident, got electrocuted, or injured, she wouldn't know where to turn. She can't use the phone any longer.'

I told him I thought that must be hard, and that simple comment hit a nerve.

'Hard? People don't get it!' he replied, bemused. 'I hardly interact with anybody, other than for things like this interview and other official matters. Neighbours say, "Oh, Ray, it must be so difficult" – but it's all platitudes. I always say it's like when you've had a death in the family, people just don't know how to talk to you, and it's the same with this. You lose touch with the world.'

After a while, Ray told me how, a few months ago, Andy had taken Pam away for a night, just to give him a bit of a break.

'He took his mother over to Manchester, just before Christmas, for a break for me, only for a day, but she stayed overnight, and they went shopping,' he told me. 'Anyway, I thought, I can't be bothered cooking just for myself tonight. I do absolutely all the cooking and housework. So, I thought, I'll ring up Amy's coffee shop – on Thursday and Friday each week, they do tapas. So, I rang up on the Wednesday, and I said, "Is it possible to have a table for one, for tomorrow night?" I went in the following evening and sat down at my table for one. "I'm Billy No-Mates," I told them, because that's exactly what I felt like,' he said. 'But then Amy came right up to me, gave me a cuddle and said, "You haven't met my father, have you?" He was this older gentleman, sitting at another table, so he came and sat with me on my table, and then her husband, Rod, came and sat with us too, and suddenly I'm part of a group again, drinking wine, talking and feeling "free" for the first time in a long time. I remembered how nice it is to be able to go into a place on your own.'

Somewhere inside, Ray knew that Pam's illness was causing her to drift further and further away from the world. And,
as much as he wanted to drift with her, right to the end, he
also had a powerful need to swim back to shore and rediscover the sort of connection a part of him longed for.

Epilogue: Dear Lonely People

Dear Lonely People,

I wanted this book to be a collection of portraits of the different ways that loneliness shows up in people's lives. In his essay, 'Good Old Neon', David Foster Wallace argues that the fact that 'we're all lonely' is now almost a cliché.[1] It's not a new argument. His theory as to *why* loneliness is a default setting for most human beings relates to a mismatch between the vastness of what's inside us at any given moment and the frustratingly inadequate tools we have with which to express and share that vastness with others. 'You already know the difference between the size and speed of everything that flashes through you and the tiny inadequate bit of it all you can ever let anyone know,' he argues, 'it's as though inside you is this enormous room full of what seems like everything in the whole universe at one time or another and yet the only parts that get out have to somehow squeeze out through one of those tiny keyholes you see under the knob in older doors. As if we are all trying to see each other through these tiny keyholes.'

You might well ask, what is the value in a portrait collection of people's experiences of loneliness? Why create such an anthology of suffering? As I wrote this book, I was struck by the fact that almost everyone who asked me what I was writing about had their own personal stories of loneliness to tell. Many people were bold enough to ask outright whether their personal stories might form part of the book, and seemed eager for their experiences to be squeezed out of the keyhole so that others could *see* a part of them that had been *unseen* for so long. I think David Foster Wallace was right to say that part of the suffering in the sort of loneliness he describes can be reduced to the fact that the immense difficulty we have in sharing or articulating our experiences of it can itself become a 'component of the pain and a contributing factor in its essential horror'.[2] That does not mean that someone else's story completely maps onto our own experiences of loneliness. I don't think that any two stories of loneliness are the same. However, I believe that sharing stories can give us a sense that there are parallels, similarities, intimations of our personal experiences that help us feel as though *our* loneliness has been recognized, out there, beyond the room behind the tiny keyhole.

When I was a child, I used to love our family trips to the DIY store. We would all pile into the red Cortina estate and make our way to B&Q or Homebase. On the way home, if we were lucky, we might stop for tea at the Little Chef, and I'd order the jumbo fish finger, chips and beans, followed by an ice cream sundae with chocolate sauce. Something about the layout of the DIY stores captivated me. I would get lost exploring the labyrinth of aisles. I'd systematically look for the front doors so that I could ring the doorbells, then I'd find the windows, the lighting, the showers, the beds and the sofas. My brother, sister and I would visit the mock bathrooms, kitchens, living rooms and dining rooms. We'd pick our favourite and get lost in an imaginary world of 'playing house' among these luxurious replica rooms. We'd play hide and seek, wonder at the hundreds of different lamps and lampshades that illuminated the lighting section, and disagree about which sofa was the most comfortable.

In the painting and decorating section, it was always the Dulux colour chart that captured my attention. I simply couldn't comprehend that there were so many different shades of any given colour. In orange alone, there were shades such as 'soft peach', 'orange fizz', 'apricot crush', 'Moroccan flame' and 'tangerine twist'. Green could be anything from 'Nordic spa', 'fresh sage' and 'pixie green' to 'emerald glade' or 'bamboo stem'. I particularly marvelled at how a colour I knew simply as 'black' could be separated into 'traffic black', 'jet black', 'volcanic black' or 'satin black'. And it wasn't just marketing bullshit. I could empirically verify with my own eyes that the different shades of any given colour were indeed distinguishable. And, somehow, they were infinite.

I see this book as a Dulux colour chart of some of the many shades of loneliness that characterize people's lives. Of course, I haven't seen all of the billions of shades of loneliness that exist out there. I have only witnessed and experienced the very tip of the iceberg. But, by capturing them in these stories, I hope that I have at least begun to chronicle the different ways that humans experience something like loneliness. I have tried to loosely categorize the stories into sections that reflect some of the broader ways loneliness seems to impact people's lives. I appreciate that, in doing so, I have done little more than identify a few of the infinite oranges, greens or blacks on the colour chart of loneliness.

Of course, our lived experiences are rarely a simple reflection of the artificially isolated shades of loneliness that something like a Dulux colour chart depicts. The stories I've presented here are more like a multicoloured ball of plasticine, where different shades of loneliness are all mashed together in a messy, abstract way, and some colours are more prevalent or dominant than others. I'm not sure it's possible, or desirable, to surgically separate out these colours and shades, because, well, that's not how life happens. I like to think of these stories as opportunities for circumambulation of the different multicoloured balls of plasticine that reflect people's experiences of loneliness. I encourage readers to move around the experiences presented in the stories, in the same way you might approach curious examination of a sculpture or statue.

I didn't think, at the outset, that such a central thread would also be chronicling the undeniable procession of loneliness that has evidently followed me through my life. Reading my own words in the pages of this book has helped me to appreciate that I have been, at many times in my life, undeniably very lonely indeed. Perhaps you have had a similar experience. In just over forty years, it seems that I have had more brushes with loneliness in various guises than I would have cared to admit – until now. And, looking ahead, I shudder to think how many more times I am destined to hear the whisper of loneliness in my ear or feel its presence beside me. Now, perhaps, I at least understand it better.

Along the way, certain books have provided me with a sanctuary, where I've managed to feel as though someone understood, acknowledged and at least partially articulated my personal struggles with loneliness. I have built what feels like a pseudo relationship with the human consciousness and intelligence behind those books. One of them is John Bowlby's *Attachment and Loss*, in which the author talks about how our internal worlds reconfigure themselves to adapt to the emotional or relational landscape in which we find ourselves.[3] He uses terms such as 'internal working models' to describe how our thoughts, emotions and behaviour evolve into a rulebook or script that we carry around in our heads about how best to negotiate relationships based upon our experiences of trying to get close to people and feel safe and loved. I was struck by how incredibly simple, yet complex, his hypothesis is. It makes sense to me that, if we have grown up amid intimate relationships that somehow reinforce the idea that the world isn't going to be there for us when we are vulnerable, then we will, in a Darwinian sense, evolve to survive in that sort of terrain.

The complexity, detail and richness with which Bowlby describes *how* we evolve was eye-opening for me. We develop expectations about whether we are loveable, about the likelihood that others will accept and welcome us with open arms, whether love is unconditional or something to be earned, the extent to which we are able to trust, whether we believe the world truly wants to know us as we are, whether we feel safer relying upon ourselves or others, and whether we close our doors, run for the hills or become aggressive when life presents us with hardships.

The 1980s movie *The Elephant Man* is based on the life of Joseph Merrick, who was heavily disfigured and was mistreated while scraping a living as a 'side-show freak'. Behind Merrick's monstrous facade, the movie portrays him, in an emotional and intellectual sense, as a human being like everyone else, but one who lives a life of emotional torture because of the relational barriers his disfigurement presents. There is a scene in the movie that particularly resonates with me and about which I had completely forgotten until I started writing this book. Joseph Merrick is walking down the street and, as he walks, a sea of people in front of him on the pavement part, a bit like Moses parting the Red Sea as the Israelites escaped the pursuing Egyptians. The people around Merrick recoil because they are afraid of him, repulsed by him, and are instinctively wary. You can see it written all over their faces as they step back, aghast. What strikes me in the scene is how this is such a painful assault on Joseph Merrick's sense of self. He is deeply wounded – it's visible in his eyes – and he finally reaches a point where he can no longer tolerate the level of disconnection to which the world has subjected him. He screams, indignantly, at the top of his voice, 'I AM NOT AN ANIMAL!' And the people further recoil.

That scene makes me think about the 'internal working model' concept I described above. Some of us are born into a world where we are deeply wounded by a sense that, for whatever reason, the world doesn't want to get close to us, maybe it even runs away from us. I don't have to be a genius to realize that I'm probably one of those people. When I experienced the barren, isolated relationship I shared with Dad, for example, one of the conclusions I reached was that there might be something about me that was inherently unlovable – grotesque, even – and that was the reason he felt he needed to keep his distance. I constructed the warped idea that I probably wasn't inherently loveable 'just because', and that I needed to earn any love, acceptance and security I might have craved. I have learned how to earn it by doing things like taking on the challenges of parentification, becoming the listener, or serving the emotional needs of others at the expense of my own. And, as an operational map, there's a high chance that's going to lead you right into the heartlands of loneliness.

It's also a lonely admission that I have managed to find solace in an academic text like Bowlby's, but I have always felt that the work reflects an older, wiser, comforting intelligence in my life that I have often longed for – exactly the sort of presence that's so important in protecting us from the turbulent seas of loneliness and isolation that life has in store. Thanks to his work, I have at least felt more seen, as though the many skirmishes I've had with loneliness have somehow been acknowledged by *someone*, even if that acknowledgement has a technical, theoretical tone. I hope that somewhere, somehow, this book might provide someone with similar comfort.

Of course, although I have taken sustenance from the fact that theories and ideas have helped me to articulate my loneliness, it doesn't fully alleviate it. Immersing myself in research and speaking in depth to people with similar experiences of loneliness sometimes feels a little like having a limb lopped off and eloquently narrating the whole experience from an anatomical, biological or clinical perspective. What's missing, still, is the sort of human connection we all need, like someone holding your hand, making soothing and comforting noises or giving you the sense that they genuinely care about how distressing the experience might be for you.

The poet Muriel Rukeyser once wrote about the fact that the universe is not made of atoms, but stories.[4] With that in mind, I have written stories about experiences of loneliness that have touched me personally or have touched the lives of people I have been privileged enough to know. Some of those experiences may feel familiar to you and some of them may not. Some of the shades of loneliness I have presented are a brutal kind of loneliness, others more like the distant bark of a fox in the night. For some, it's constant, permanently in the background, like an unwelcome presence that follows you home on a dark night. For others, it's more like an unexpected air raid, swooping into your life unannounced, wreaking havoc and devastation. Sometimes it quietly sneaks in the back door, and sometimes it crashes through the living-room wall.

The value of stories in relation to loneliness is, I think, partly connected to empathy – the ability to share, appreciate and understand the affective, cognitive, existential and experiential worlds of other people. And perhaps by being more aware of our own and others' experiences and stories of loneliness, and by sharing those experiences, some sort of mutual empathy can be found. Stories are and always have been valued across all cultural groups as an essential way to foster understanding. In the end, I think empathy may be one of the most important antidotes we have for loneliness.

However, there is always the argument that perhaps we shouldn't be too hasty in looking for an antidote. That loneliness may be an inevitable part of almost everyone's life story hints at the fact that perhaps we are fated to encounter it, a bit like death itself.

You might put that down to a design flaw, as David Foster Wallace did – the idea that there's just too much going on within us to ever communicate it all adequately enough to feel known through the keyholes that offer others the tiniest glimpse of what's inside. However, author and Jungian analyst Lisa Marchiano has a different perspective, and, in her podcast *This Jungian Life*, she recently described loneliness as a 'crucible for spiritual development'. She argues that the times in her life when she has been intensely lonely have undoubtedly been extremely painful to the point that they felt intolerable. But, she continues, 'they were also times in my life when I had to reach into myself, be with myself, and learn to rely on my own inner resources'. In the darkness that is loneliness, there is often something awaiting us, and it may be a precious lesson in our relationship with ourselves.

With gratitude,

Sam

Further Reading

Barrett, D., *Supernormal Stimuli: How Primal Urges Overran their Evolutionary Purpose* (New York: W. W. Norton & Company, 2010).

Booker, C., *The Seven Basic Plots: Why We Tell Stories* (London: A & C Black, 2004).

Bowlby, E. J. M., *Attachment,* volume one of the *Attachment and Loss* trilogy (New York: Basic Books, 1969).

Bowlby, E. J. M., *Separation: Anxiety and Anger,* volume two of the *Attachment and Loss* trilogy (New York: Basic Books, 1973).

Bowlby, E. J. M., *Loss: Sadness and Depression,* volume three of the *Attachment and Loss* trilogy (New York: Basic Books, 1980).

Carotenuto, A., *Eros and Pathos: Shades of Love and Suffering* (Toronto: Inner City Books, 1989).

Carter, R., *Multiplicity: The New Science of Personality, Identity, and the Self* (London: Little, Brown, 2008).

Dowling, C., *The Cinderella Complex: Women's Hidden Fear of Independence* (London: Fontana Press, 1982).

Estes, C. P., *Women Who Run With the Wolves: Myths and Stories of the Wild Woman Archetype* (New York: Ballantine Books, 1995).

Frankl, V. E., *Man's Search for Meaning* (New York: Simon and Schuster, 1985).

Gawande, A., *Being Mortal: Medicine and What Matters in the End* (New York: Metropolitan Books, 2014).

Grosz, S., *The Examined Life: How We Lose and Find Ourselves* (London: Vintage, 2013).

Hollis, J., *The Middle Passage: From Misery to Meaning in Midlife* (Toronto: Inner City Books, 1993).

Hollis, J., *Under Saturn's Shadow: The Wounding and Healing of Men* (Toronto: Inner City Books, 1994).

Paris, G., *Heartbreak: New Approaches to Healing – Recovering from Lost Love and Mourning* (Minneapolis: Hillcrest Media Group, 2011).

Rothman, J. and Feinberg, S., *Every Body: An Honest and Open Look at Sex from Every Angle* (New York: Little, Brown, 2021).

Van der Kolk, B., *The Body Keeps the Score: Brain, Mind, and Body in the Healing of Trauma* (New York: Penguin, 2014).

Wallace, D. F., *Oblivion: Stories* (London: Little, Brown, 2004).

Wallace, D. F., *Consider the Lobster: And Other Essays* (London: Little, Brown, 2005).

Wallace, D. F., *The Pale King* (London: Little, Brown, 2011).

Wallace, D. F., *Brief Interviews with Hideous Men* (London: Little, Brown, 2012).

Yanagihara, H., *A Little Life* (London: Picador, 2015).

Acknowledgements

I would like to thank the friends, family and colleagues with whom I've shared deep and meaningful relationships, experiences and conversations about themes that crop up in this book. Special thanks to Mum, Dad, Em, Joe, Natalie, Professor Malcolm Johnson, Dr Chao Fang, Dr Jana Kralova, Dr Ceri Brown, Dr Ioannis Costas Batlle, Dr Ben Rockett, Caroline Hickman and my friend Dana Ben Halim. You may not know it, but our conversations over many years have been a huge part of helping me to explore being human.

Thanks also to the people who generously granted me the privilege of exploring their inner worlds with them, helping to sculpt the stories that form the essence of this book. The conversations, relationships and experiences we shared together are something I will never forget. They were a beautiful gift that has taught me so much and that I hope will keep on giving as your stories reverberate.

Thanks to my agent, Doug Young, at PEW Literary, for helping me conceptualize this book, make it into a reality, and simply for being such a quietly supportive, wise presence along the way. Sincere thanks are also extended to Andrea Henry and Marissa Constantinou at Picador; your editorial expertise, enthusiasm and passion for the stories and subject matter have been invaluable and I am grateful for your kind, supportive and deeply human approach to the project from the outset. I couldn't have asked for better editorial support.

236 ALL THE LONELY PEOPLE

Finally, I want to thank Alex, for being the person who has listened most to these stories over the last few years. Thank you for genuinely wanting to hear the stories, night after night, and for offering me your valuable reflections on endless 'midnight drives'. I will never forget how we drove deep into the night and talked about the stories together, what they mean for us, how they make us feel, what they teach us and what it is to be human.

Notes and Sources

Introduction

1 Wodehouse, P. G., *Very Good, Jeeves!* (London: Arrow Books, 2008), reprinted ed. p. 152.

2 Gawande, A., *Being Mortal: Illness, Medicine, and What Matters in the End* (New York: Metropolitan Books, 2014), p. 55.

3 Roth, P., *Everyman* (London: Jonathan Cape, 2006). p. 76.

4 Carr, S. and Fang, C., 'A gradual separation from the world: a qualitative exploration of existential loneliness in old age', *Ageing & Society*, 2021, pp. 1–21.

5 Wallace, D. F., cited in Howard, G., *Infinite Jester*, Elle 11 (Issue 6), 1996, p. 58.

6 Jung, C. G., *Memories, Dreams, Reflections* (London: Vintage, 2011), pp. 114–45.

7 Hicks-Wilson, D., *Small Cures* (Kansas City: Andrews McMeel, 2021).

8 Lee, T., 'Skilled listening and writing for story: From reminiscence to story-work with elders' stories', *Educational Gerontology*, 42(6), 2016, pp. 423–30.

Part One: RELATIONSHIPS

1 Larsson, H., Rämgård, M. and Bolmsjö, I., 'Older persons' existential loneliness, as interpreted by their significant others – an interview study', *BMC geriatrics*, 17(1), 2017, pp. 1–9.

2 Jung, C. J., *Collected Works: Civilisation in Transition*, Vol. 10 (London: Routledge and Kegan Paul, 1964).

3 Hollis, J., *The Middle Passage: From Misery to Meaning in Midlife* (Toronto: Inner City Books, 1993), pp. 71–2.

4 Keene, G., cited in Rothman, J. and Feinberg, S., *Every Body: An Honest and Open Look at Sex from Every Angle* (New York: Little, Brown, 2021). P. 153.

5 Pinkola Estés, C., *Women Who Run with the Wolves* (London: Rider, 2008).

6 Hollis, J., *Under Saturn's Shadow: The Wounding and Healing of Men* (Toronto: Inner City Books, 1994), pp. 83–100.

Part Two: INVISIBILITY

1 Ferguson, H., 'Therapeutic journeys: The car as a vehicle for working with children and families and theorising practice', *Journal of Social Work Practice*, 24(2), 2010, pp. 121–38.

2 Capstick, A. and Clegg, D., 'Behind the stiff upper lip: War narratives of older men with dementia', *Journal of War & Culture Studies*, 6(3), 2013, pp. 239–54.

3 Dowling, C., *The Cinderella Complex: Women's Hidden Fear of Independence* (London: Fontana Press, 1982).

4 Carter, R., *Multiplicity: The new science of personality, identity, and the self* (London: Little, Brown, 2008), p. 23.

5 Brine, J., 'The everyday classificatory practices of selective schooling: a fifty-year retrospective', *International Studies in Sociology of Education*, 16(1), 2006, pp. 37–55.

6 Bartky, S. L., *Femininity and Domination: Studies in the Phenomenology of Oppression* (Oxford: Routledge, 2015), p. 22.

7 Paris, G., *Heartbreak: New Approaches to Healing* (Minneapolis: Hillcrest Media Group, 2011), p. 6.

8 Ibid, p. 77.

9 Carotenuto, A., *Eros and Pathos: Shades of Love and Suffering* (Toronto: Inner City Books, 1989), p. 82.

10 van der Kolk, B., *The Body Keeps the Score: Brain, Mind, and Body in the Healing of Trauma* (New York: Penguin, 2014), p. 234.

11 van der Kolk, B. A. and Fisler, R., 'Dissociation and the fragmentary nature of traumatic memories: Overview and exploratory study', *Journal of Traumatic Stress*, 8(4), 1995, pp. 505–25.

12 Frankl, V. E., *Man's Search for Meaning* (New York: Simon and Schuster, 1985), p. 36.

Part Three: ESCAPE

1 Khawaja, N. G., White, K. M., Schweitzer, R. and Greenslade, J., 'Difficulties and coping strategies of Sudanese refugees: A qualitative approach', *Transcultural Psychiatry*, 45(3), 2008, pp. 489–512.

2 Fozooni, B., 'Afghanistan, cricket and fairy tales: A critical analysis of Out of the Ashes', *South Asian History and Culture*, 6(2), 2015, pp. 204–22.

3 Sauvageau, A. and Racette, S., 'Agonal sequences in a filmed suicidal hanging: Analysis of respiratory and movement responses to asphyxia by hanging', *Journal of Forensic Sciences*, 52(4), 2007, pp. 957–9.

4 Battle, A. O., 'Group therapy for survivors of suicide', *Crisis: The Journal of Crisis Intervention and Suicide Prevention*, 1984, p. 54.

5 Bonnewyn, A., Shah, A., Bruffaerts, R., Schoevaerts, K., Rober, P., Van Parys, H. and Demyttenaere, K., 'Reflections of older adults on the process preceding their suicide attempt: A qualitative approach', *Death Studies*, 38(9), 2014, pp. 612–18.

6 Nelson-Becker, H. and Victor, C., 'Dying alone and lonely dying: Media discourse and pandemic conditions', *Journal of Aging Studies*, 55, 2020, article 100878.

7   Johnson, M. and Walker, J. eds., *Spiritual Dimensions of Ageing* (Cambridge: Cambridge University Press, 2016), p. 198.

8   Lipsky, D., interview with David Foster Wallace, *Rolling Stone* 1064, 30 October 2008.

9   Wallace, D. F., 'Big Red Son', in *Consider the Lobster: And Other Essays* (London: Little, Brown, 2005), p. 14.

10 British Board of Film Classification summary of research report at https://www.bbfc.co.uk/about-us/news/children-see-pornography-as-young-as-seven-new-report-finds [accessed 10 February 2023].

11 Barrett, D., *Supernormal Stimuli: How Primal Urges Overran their Evolutionary Purpose* (New York: W. W. Norton & Company, 2010).

12 See https://www.youtube.com/watch?v=NbP_ehYHfsk [accessed 15 September 2022].

13 Wallace, D. F., 'Big Red Son', in *Consider the Lobster: And Other Essays* (London: Little, Brown, 2005), p. 14.

14 Zitzman, S. T. and Butler, M. H., 'Wives' experience of husbands' pornography use and concomitant deception as an attachment threat in the adult pair-bond relationship', *Sexual Addiction & Compulsivity*, 16(3), 2009, pp. 210–40.

15 Basu, D., 'Ah, Look at All the Lonely People . . . Will social psychiatry please stand up for ministering to loneliness?', *World Social Psychiatry*, 3(1), 2021, p. 1.

16 Barreto, M., van Breen, J., Victor, C., Hammond, C., Eccles, A., Richins, M. T. and Qualter, P., 'Exploring the nature and variation of the stigma associated with loneliness', *Journal of Social and Personal Relationships*, 39(9), 2022, pp. 2658–2679.

17 Wallace, D. F., *The Pale King* (London: Penguin, 2011), p. 67.

Part Four: OUTSIDERS

1 Fang, C., 'Dynamics of Chinese Shidu parents' vulnerability in old age: A qualitative study', *Journal of Population Ageing*, 15, 2022, pp. 99–119.

2 Olofsson, J., Rämgård, M., Sjögren-Forss, K. and Bramhagen, A. C., 'Older migrants' experience of existential loneliness', *Nursing Ethics*, 28(7–8), 2021, pp. 1183-93.

3 Grosz, S., *The Examined Life: How We Lose and Find Ourselves* (London: Vintage, 2013), p. 17.

4 Olofsson, J., Rämgård, M., Sjögren-Forss, K. and Bramhagen, A. C., 'Older migrants' experience of existential loneliness', *Nursing Ethics*, 28(7–8), 2021, pp. 1183–93.

5 Yanagihara, H., *A Little Life* (London: Picador, 2015), p. 341.

6 Chiu, M., Rahman, F., Vigod, S., Lau, C., Cairney, J. and Kurdyak, P., 'Mortality in single fathers compared with single mothers and partnered parents: A population-based cohort study', *The Lancet Public Health*, 3(3), 2018, pp. e115–e123.

7 Hollis, J., *The Middle Passage: From Misery to Meaning in Midlife* (Toronto: Inner City Books, 1993), p. 41.

8 Kabeer, N., 'Social exclusion, poverty and discrimination towards an analytical framework', *IDS Bulletin*, 31(4), 2000, pp. 83–97.

9 Kovaleva, M., Spangler, S., Clevenger, C. and Hepburn, K., 'Chronic stress, social isolation, and perceived loneliness in dementia caregivers', *Journal of Psychosocial Nursing and Mental Health Services*, 56(10), 2018, pp. 36–43.

Epilogue

1 Wallace, D. F., 'Good Old Neon', in *Oblivion: Stories* (London: Little, Brown, 2004), p. 175.

2 Wallace, D. F., 'The Depressed Person', in *Brief Interviews with Hideous Men* (London: Little, Brown, 2001).

3 Bowlby, E. J. M., *Attachment*, volume one of the *Attachment and Loss* trilogy (New York: Random House, 2008).

4 Rukeyser, M., cited in Kaufman, J. E. and Herzog, A., eds. *The Collected Poems of Muriel Rukeyser*. (Pittsburgh: University of Pittsburgh Press, 2005), p. 467.

Sam Carr is a psychologist and social scientist with the Department of Education and Centre for Death & Society at the University of Bath. He was the director of The Loneliness Project, a partnership between the University of Bath and Guild Living, a later-living retirement community provider. He has written extensively in the media about his research and has spoken about it on local and national radio, as well as being an academic expert on various television documentaries. Sam lives in rural Wiltshire with his son and their cat.